# EXPLORING

# ANCIENT
# CIVILIZATIONS

# 1

## Aboriginal Culture – Aryans

Marshall Cavendish
 Sydney

Marshall Cavendish
99 White Plains Road
Tarrytown, New York 10591-9001

www.marshallcavendish.com

*Consultants:* Daud Ali, School of Oriental and African Studies, University of London; Michael Brett, School of Oriental and African Studies, London; John Chinnery, School of Oriental and African Studies, London; Philip de Souza; Joann Fletcher; Anthony Green; Peter Groff, Department of Philosophy, Bucknell University; Mark Handley, History Department, University College London; Anders Karlsson, School of Oriental and African Studies, London; Alan Leslie, Glasgow University Archaeology Research Department; Michael E. Smith, Department of Anthropology, University at Albany; Matthew Spriggs, Head of School of Archaeology and Anthropology, Australian National University

*Contributing authors:* Richard Balkwill, Richard Burrows, Peter Chrisp, Richard Dargie, Steve Eddy, Clive Gifford, Jen Green, Peter Hicks, Robert Hull, Jonathan Ingoldby, Pat Levy, Steven Maddocks, John Malam, Saviour Pirotta, Stewart Ross, Sean Sheehan, Jane Shuter

WHITE-THOMSON PUBLISHING
*Editors:* Alex Woolf and Steven Maddocks
*Design:* Derek Lee
*Cartographer:* Peter Bull Design
*Picture Research:* Glass Onion Pictures
*Indexer:* Fiona Barr

MARSHALL CAVENDISH
*Editor:* Thomas McCarthy
*Editorial Director:* Paul Bernabeo
*Production Manager:* Michael Esposito

Library of Congress Cataloging-in-Publication Data
Exploring ancient civilizations.
    p. cm.
Includes bibliographical references and indexes.
  ISBN 0-7614-7456-0 (set : alk. paper) -- ISBN 0-7614-7457-9 (v. 1 : alk. paper) -- ISBN 0-7614-7458-7 (v. 2 : alk. paper) -- ISBN 0-7614-7459-5 (v. 3 : alk. paper) -- ISBN 0-7614-7460-9 (v. 4 : alk. paper) -- ISBN 0-7614-7461-7 (v. 5 : alk. paper) -- ISBN 0-7614-7462-5 (v. 6 : alk. paper) -- ISBN 0-7614-7463-3 (v. 7 : alk. paper) -- ISBN 0-7614-7464-1 (v. 8 : alk. paper) -- ISBN 0-7614-7465-X (v. 9 : alk. paper) -- ISBN 0-7614-7466-8 (v. 10 : alk. paper) -- ISBN 0-7614-7467-6 (v. 11 : alk. paper)
  1. Civilization, Ancient--Encyclopedias.
  CB311.E97 2004
  930'.03--dc21

                    2003041224

ISBN 0-7614-7456-0 (set)
ISBN 0-7614-7457-9 (vol. 1)

Printed and bound in China

07 06 05 04 03  5 4 3 2 1

**ILLUSTRATION CREDITS**
**AKG London:** 19 (Erich Lessing), 23, 33 (Erich Lessing), 35 (Erich Lessing), 36 (Erich Lessing), 37 (Erich Lessing), 41, 51, 69.
**Art Archive:** 27 (Accademia San Luca, Rome / Dagli Orti), 42 (Victoria and Albert Museum, London / Eileen Tweedy), 61 (Navy Historical Service, Vincennes, France / Dagli Orti), 70 (Hittite Museum, Ankara / Dagli Orti).
**Bridgeman Art Library:** 16 (National Library of Australia, Canberra), 17 (Stapleton Collection, UK), 20, 21 (Birmingham Museums and Art Gallery, UK), 22 (Index), 24 (National Archaeological Museum, Athens), 25 (Peter Willi), 28 (Cincinnati Art Museum), 29, 31 (Ashmolean Museum, Oxford), 32 (Musée du Louvre, Paris), 38 (Archaeological Museum, Istanbul), 39 (Statens Museum for Kunst, Copenhagen), 44, 55 (Ashmolean Mueum, Oxford), 56 (Museo Archeologico Nazionale, Naples), 57 (Hartlepool Museum Service, Cleveland, UK), 59 (Giraudon), 60 (Townely Hall Art Gallery and Museum, Burnley, UK), 65 (Central Saint Martin's College of Art and Design, London), 66, 67 (Kunsthistorisches Museum, Vienna), 68 (Vatican Museums and Galleries), 71 (Giraudon), 72 (Museum of Fine Arts, Houston), 73 (British Museum, London), 74 (British Library, London), 77 (National Museum of India, New Delhi).
**British Library, London:** 76.
**Corbis:** 64 (Paul Almasy).
**Joann Fletcher:** 62.
**Japan Broadcasting Corporation:** 78.
**Mary Evans Picture Library:** 43.
**Petrie Museum of Egyptian Archaeology:** 63.
**South American Pictures:** 51.
**Werner Forman Archive:** 15, 26 (British Museum, London), 45: (Egyptian Museum, Cairo), 46, 47 (Egyptian Museum, Cairo), 48: (Shaanxi Provincial Museum, Xian, China), 52, 53 (Maxwell Museum of Anthropology, Albuquerque), 58 (British Museum, London).

# Contents

# Set Contents

## VOLUME 4

## VOLUME 5

## VOLUME 6

## VOLUME 7

## VOLUME 8

# Thematic Contents

## CIVILIZATIONS AND PEOPLES

## BIOGRAPHIES OF PEOPLE, LEGENDARY FIGURES, AND DEITIES

## PLACES

## PHILOSOPHY, RELIGION, AND MYTHOLOGY

## WRITINGS

# Introduction

Those who make history, those who write it, and those who read it may agree on little, but they hold at least one common assumption: the past matters. Specifically, the past matters to the present. This assumption underlies the making of *Exploring Ancient Civilizations*.

One reason people study the civilizations and cultures of the ancient world is to learn why the past at times seems so different from the present. Why did people who lived in earlier societies think and act as they did? Why were some of their attitudes so unlike those of the present day? Sometimes one finds illuminating answers to these questions. Just as often, however, satisfactory answers cannot be found. Still, the very absence of a good answer may be equally illuminating, since learning that people can differ profoundly about matters of fundamental significance is an important lesson for a student of any age.

Differences, however, are merely a part of the picture. Another reason for studying the past is to learn how it was similar to the present. Observing the continuity of human impulses, motivations, and actions over the course of centuries and millennia can be comforting or dismaying or even startling. Almost three thousand years ago a Hebrew sage wrote, "There is nothing new under the sun." Even if he was right and all roads have already been trod, some of the places the roads lead to are more desirable as destinations than are others. Study of the past can help an attentive student in the difficult but profitable business of distinguishing the more desirable from the less so.

Establishing an end date for the ancient world is both an arbitrary and essential component in constructing such a reference work as this. The choice of the year 500 of the present era as a more or less inflexible finish line permits coverage of a wide spectrum of interesting peoples and societies while also necessarily placing other equally important persons, cultures, and phenomena out of reach. Nevertheless, the fact remains that these volumes offer a glimpse of the varied responses to the challenges of life that ancient peoples from all over the globe devised over a span of roughly seven thousand years. Some civilizations were vast and enduring; others rose and fell, figuratively speaking, with the speed of a summer shower. Of some (such as ancient Rome and China), much is known; of others, only little. Thanks to the labors of historians, archaeologists, and other scholars, however, hardly a year goes by without further enrichment of humankind's knowledge of its past. The writers, editors, and publisher of *Exploring Ancient Civilizations* hope that this work will give you, its readers, a taste of—and *for*—these wondrous riches.

# Reader's Guide

This encyclopedia contains a total of 249 articles in 10 volumes, covering all aspects of the ancient world. The entries are grouped under the following themes: civilizations and peoples; biographies of people, legendary figures, and deities; places; philosophy, religion, and mythology; and writings. There are also cross-cultural articles on general topics such as art, education, and technology. The Thematic Contents, on pages 8 to 11 in this volume, categorize the articles by these themes.

The period of time encompassed by this encyclopedia is approximately 6500 BCE to 500 CE. Broadly speaking, this span covers the period that begins with the development of writing and farming and the building of the first cities and ends with the fall of the Roman Empire and the start of the Dark Ages in Europe.

All articles contain at least one panel. There are three types of panels in all. Feature panels highlight aspects of particular interest in the subject under discussion. Biographical panels offer brief accounts of significant individuals not covered in the main articles. Birth and death dates, where known, are included alongside the person's name. Quotation panels provide illuminating quotes from contemporary sources.

As an easy-reference guide, the articles have been color-coded by geographical region. Cross-cultural articles have their own separate color code. The color codes are as follows.

- ■ Cross-cultural
- ■ Africa
- ■ Americas
- ■ Eastern Asia
- ■ Europe
- ■ Oceania and Australia
- ■ Southern Asia
- ■ Western Asia

Articles about civilizations and peoples always include a map and a time line to help locate the civilization in both place and time. All articles conclude with a list of cross-references to other, related articles.

Each volume concludes with a glossary and an index. Volume 11, the final volume, contains a time line of the ancient world, a comprehensive glossary, resources for further study, Internet resources, a map list and index, a group of thematic indexes, and a comprehensive index.

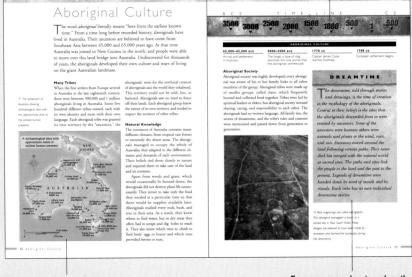

*All articles on civilizations contain a time line.*

*All articles on civilizations contain a map.*

*Color code tells you which part of the world is being dealt with in this article.*

*Feature panels give details of a particular aspect of the subject.*

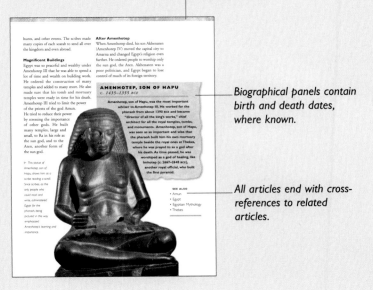

*Biographical panels contain birth and death dates, where known.*

*All articles end with cross-references to related articles.*

# Aboriginal Culture

The word *aboriginal* literally means "here from the earliest known time." From a time long before recorded history, aboriginals have lived in Australia. Their ancestors are believed to have come from Southeast Asia between 45,000 and 65,000 years ago. At that time Australia was joined to New Guinea in the north, and people were able to move over this land bridge into Australia. Undiscovered for thousands of years, the aboriginals developed their own culture and ways of living on the giant Australian landmass.

## Many Tribes

When the first settlers from Europe arrived in Australia in the late eighteenth century, there were between 300,000 and 1 million aboriginals living in Australia. Some five hundred different tribes existed, each with its own identity and most with their own language. Each aboriginal tribe was granted its own territory by the "ancestors," the aboriginals' term for the mythical creators of aboriginals and the world they inhabited. This territory could not be sold, lost, or bartered. Aboriginals saw no need to fence off their lands. Each aboriginal group knew the extent of its own territory and tended to respect the territory of other tribes.

## Natural Knowledge

The continent of Australia contains many different climates, from tropical rain forests to extremely dry desert areas. The aboriginals managed to occupy the whole of Australia; they adapted to the different climates and demands of each environment. Their beliefs tied them closely to nature and required them to take care of the land and its contents.

Apart from weeds and grass, which would occasionally be burned down, the aboriginals did not destroy plant life unnecessarily. They strove to take only the food they needed at a particular time so that there would be supplies available later. Aboriginals studied every rock, bush, and tree in their area. As a result, they knew where to find water, but in dry areas they often had to scrape and dig holes to reach it. They also knew which trees to climb to find birds' eggs or honey and which trees provided berries or nuts.

▼ *The settlement of Australia, showing archaeological sites with the approximate date of the earliest human presence.*

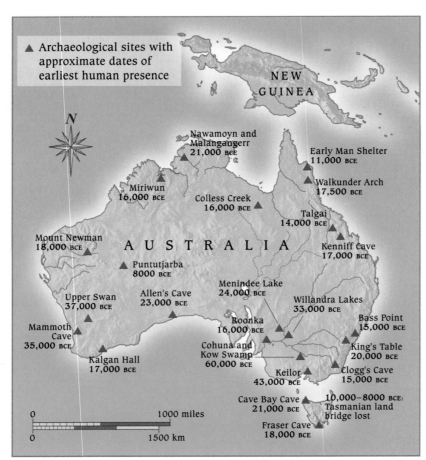

▲ Archaeological sites with approximate dates of earliest human presence

NEW GUINEA

N

Nawamoyn and Malangangerr 21,000 BCE

Early Man Shelter 11,000 BCE

Miriwun 16,000 BCE

Walkunder Arch 17,500 BCE

Colless Creek 16,000 BCE

Talgai 14,000 BCE

Mount Newman 18,000 BCE

AUSTRALIA

Kenniff Cave 17,000 BCE

Puntutjarba 8000 BCE

Menindee Lake 24,000 BCE

Upper Swan 37,000 BCE

Allen's Cave 23,000 BCE

Willandra Lakes 33,000 BCE

Bass Point 15,000 BCE

Mammoth Cave 35,000 BCE

Roonka 16,000 BCE

King's Table 20,000 BCE

Kalgan Hall 17,000 BCE

Cohuna and Kow Swamp 60,000 BCE

Clogg's Cave 15,000 BCE

Keilor 43,000 BCE

Cave Bay Cave 21,000 BCE

10,000–8000 BCE: Tasmanian land bridge lost

Fraser Cave 18,000 BCE

0          1000 miles

0          1500 km

## ABORIGINAL CULTURE

**65,000–45,000 BCE**
Arrival and settlement in Australia.

**5000–3000 BCE**
The dingo, a type of dog, becomes the only animal that the aboriginals domesticate.

**1770 CE**
Captain James Cook reaches Australia.

**1788 CE**
European settlement begins.

### Aboriginal Society

Aboriginal society was highly developed; every aboriginal was aware of his or her family links to all other members of the group. Aboriginal tribes were made up of smaller groups, called clans, which frequently hunted and collected food together. Tribes were led by spiritual leaders or elders, but aboriginal society stressed sharing, caring, and responsibility to each other. The aboriginals had no written language. All family ties, the stories of dreamtime, and the tribe's rules and customs were memorized and passed down from generation to generation.

### DREAMTIME

The dreamtime, told through stories and drawings, is the time of creation in the mythology of the aboriginals. Central to their beliefs is the idea that the aboriginals descended from or were created by ancestors. Some of the ancestors were human; others were animals and plants or the wind, rain, and sun. Ancestors moved around the land following certain paths. They never died but merged with the natural world at sacred sites. The paths and sites link the people to the land and the past to the present. Legends of dreamtime were handed down by word of mouth and by rituals. Each tribe has its own individual dreamtime stories.

◄ Rock engravings are called petroglyphs. This aboriginal petroglyph is found at a sacred site in New South Wales. These designs are believed to have been made by ancestors who formed the landscape during the dreamtime.

▶ *This nineteenth-century watercolor painting shows an aboriginal ceremony called a corroboree, which involved songs, music, and dancing, often expressing stories and beliefs from dreamtime.*

### Living off the Land

The aboriginals did not sow crops or rear animals for food. Instead, aboriginal men hunted larger animals, while the women searched for and collected grass seeds, grubs, berries, small lizards, and edible roots, such as the yam. Women collected that day's harvest in a wooden bowl or a string sack called a dilly bag. Food was shared among group members and either cooked in the ashes of a fire or eaten raw. The aboriginals were among the world's first bakers; they mixed ground seeds with a little water to make a paste that was cooked into a flat bread in the ashes of a fire.

### Art and Music

Aboriginal culture is rich, with distinctive styles of painting, stories, music, and dance. Stories from dreamtime were often told with drawings made on the ground, many of which were sacred and were not allowed to be seen by strangers. Rock and cave paintings also illustrated scenes from dreamtime and the ancestors. At the time of ceremonies and corroborees (a type of dance), aboriginals would decorate themselves with white, red, or yellow designs painted on their bodies. Instruments such as the didgeridoo and two boomerangs clapped together would provide music.

### The European Arrival

Despite their wealth of art, music, and storytelling, early settlers from Europe viewed aboriginals as savages. Tribal lands were seized by the settlers, often using force, and sacred sites were damaged or destroyed. The Europeans brought diseases with them against which the aboriginals had no natural protection. Thousands of aboriginals died from tuberculosis, smallpox, and the common cold virus. Many more died in the wars over land, as spears were no match for the Europeans' guns. Only since the latter half of the twentieth century have real attempts been made to protect aboriginal culture, to return some lands, and to respect the traditions of one of the world's longest-surviving civilizations.

# HUNTING

**B**ecause Australia is isolated from the rest of the world, its animal life did not include herd animals such as cows, sheep, and pigs. In their place were other creatures: the kangaroo, opossum, duck-billed platypus, and wallaby. Aboriginal men hunted these animals with great skill and ingenuity. The emu, a large ostrichlike bird, was often lured into a trap by playing a wooden horn. Channels were dug between streams or between swamps and streams to collect and kill eels, while nets and traps caught turtles, ducks, fish, and shellfish. Hunters often tricked kangaroos by covering themselves with mud to remove any trace of their scent.

Shaped from wood, the boomerang was a hunting weapon used by some aboriginal tribes. A sweeping throw released the boomerang at great speed to stun or kill animals or even to kill a bird in flight. However, the main hunting weapon was the long spear. Each tribe had its own type of spear, with lengths varying from four feet (1.2 m) to seventeen feet (5.2 m). Some tribes used stones to whittle down the spear end to a point. Others used sharpened fish bones, the shells of fish, or flakes of stone bound to the spear end with plant fibers.

◄ This nineteenth-century engraving shows how aboriginals in New South Wales hunted kangaroos in groups using wooden spears. A number of trees, including the blackwood and the cherry, provided wood for aboriginal spears, which were sharpened to a point using stones.

**SEE ALSO**
- Kakadu Region
- Uluru

# Achaemenids

The Achaemenids (also known as Hakhamanishiya) were the royal house of Persia, allegedly founded in the seventh century BCE by Hakhamanish, known in Greek as Achaemenes. At first the Achaemenids were vassals of the Medes. By the middle of the sixth century BCE, however, they had built up a small kingdom in the Anshan and Parsa regions on the northern coast of the Persian Gulf.

## The Great Kings

Traditionally, the first Achaemenid king of the Persians was Cyrus the Great (reigned 550–529 BCE), who was said to have had a Persian father and a Median mother. He united these two peoples and built an empire that straddled most of southwest Asia. His son, Cambyses (reigned 529–522 BCE) added Egypt to the empire before dying mysteriously in Syria.

Of all the Achaemenids, Darius I, who ruled from 521 to 486 BCE, is the best known, because the Greek historian Herodotus wrote about his reign. After his defeat by the Greeks at Marathon in 490 BCE, Darius planned to invade Greece again, but he died before he could do so.

His son Xerxes, continuing Darius's plan, defeated the Spartans at Thermopylae and burned the deserted city of Athens in 480 BCE. However, the Athenians defeated Xerxes' fleet at Salamis and his army at Plataea. Like his father, Xerxes never managed to force the Greeks to offer him earth and water, the sign of submission to the Persian emperor. Still, under Xerxes, the Persian Empire reached its greatest extent.

▼ The Achaemenid Empire, showing its expansion under successive emperors.

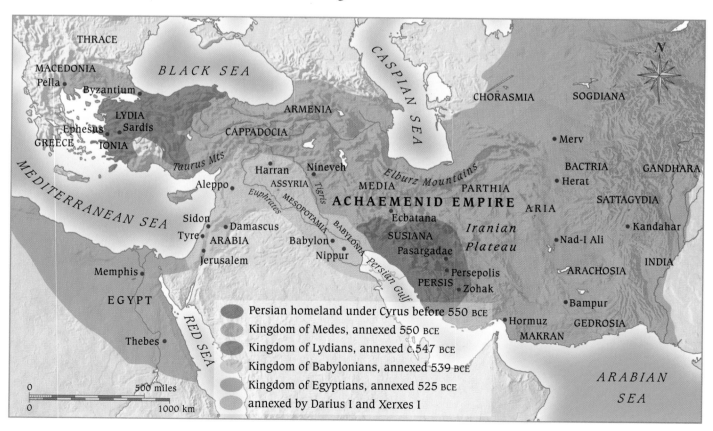

Persian homeland under Cyrus before 550 BCE
Kingdom of Medes, annexed 550 BCE
Kingdom of Lydians, annexed c.547 BCE
Kingdom of Babylonians, annexed 539 BCE
Kingdom of Egyptians, annexed 525 BCE
annexed by Darius I and Xerxes I

**3500**  **3000**  **2500**  **2000**  **1500**  **1000**  **500**  **1**  **500**

## ACHAEMENIDS

**550 BCE**

Cyrus unites the Medes and Persians.

**539 BCE**

Cyrus captures Babylon.

**515 BCE**

Darius crosses the Bosporus to attack the Scythians.

**490 BCE**

Persian expedition to Athens defeated at Marathon.

**481–480 BCE**

Xerxes invades Greece and destroys Athens but loses fleet at Salamis.

**479 BCE**

Persian army defeated at Plataea.

**464–425 BCE**

Long, peaceful reign of Artaxerxes I.

**358–338 BCE**

Persian Empire rebuilt and strengthened by Artaxerxes III.

**334 BCE**

Alexander the Great invades Persian Empire.

**330 BCE**

Alexander becomes king of Persia; end of the Achaemenid line.

### The Later Achaemenids

The royal house of Achaemenid was weakened by court intrigues and civil wars. Xerxes himself was murdered by his own *hazarapat*, or chief minister. His son Artaxerxes I (reigned 465–425 BCE) murdered his own brother to gain the throne. The empire was further weakened when civil war broke out in 401 BCE between Artaxerxes II and his brother Cyrus.

### The Fall of the Royal House

The last Achaemenid was Darius III (reigned 336–330 BCE). He had barely settled on the throne when the Macedonian king Alexander the Great invaded Persia. Darius suffered three defeats in rapid succession. Deserted by his troops, the last of the Achaemenid kings was killed by one of his own satraps.

◄ *This relief in tiles at Persepolis shows one of the Immortals, a regiment of ten thousand elite soldiers who guarded the Persian king.*

#### SEE ALSO

- Ahura Mazda • Alexander the Great
- Aryans • Athens • Babylon
- Cyrus the Great • Darius I • Herodotus
- Persepolis • Scythians • Xerxes

*During the reigns of Cyrus and Cambyses there was no fixed tribute at all, the revenue coming from gifts only; and because of his imposition of regular taxes, and other similar measures, the Persians have a saying that Darius was a tradesman, Cambyses a tyrant, and Cyrus a father — the first being out for profit wherever he could get it, the second harsh and careless of his subjects' interests, and the third, in the kindness of his heart always occupied with plans for their well-being.*

HERODOTUS, *THE HISTORIES*

# Acropolis

The Acropolis is a hill that dominates the skyline of Athens. On the Acropolis sits a cluster of temples built on top of a huge limestone rock rising five hundred feet (152 m) above the surrounding plain. In ancient times the Acropolis was the citadel of Athens and was used as a place of refuge when the city was under attack. As Athens grew in wealth and power, the Acropolis became the site of some of the most remarkable buildings and statues of the ancient world.

## History

There was a settlement on the site of the Acropolis from as early as 3500 BCE. By around 1500 BCE a palace had been built there surrounded by a defensive wall. The Acropolis was an ideal fortress for a besieged city because there was a secret water supply within the rock. When Athens began to develop into a city-state around 600 BCE, the function of the Acropolis changed. It was no longer the political and social center of the city – this moved to another part of the city called the Agora – but the Acropolis became the religious center of Athens.

In 480 BCE Athens, including the Acropolis, was sacked and badly damaged by Persian invaders. After the Persians had been driven out of Greece the following year, the city's defenses were rebuilt. However, it was another thirty years before the Acropolis was rebuilt, under the leadership of Pericles and the artistic direction of Phidias.

## The Parthenon

The new Acropolis was to be dominated by a magnficent temple called the Parthenon, 228 feet (69.5 m) long and 66 feet (20 m) high, which took fifteen years to build. In the temple's inner room, or cella, was a forty-foot (12 m) high gold and ivory statue of Athena, goddess of wisdom and protectress of Athens. She wore a long robe and a helmet, and carried a spear and shield. The statue was surrounded by forty-six columns holding up a huge roof. On the pediments at each end were marble statues, while along the sides were carved friezes of the Panathenaic festival – the most important religious celebration in Athens.

◀ *A view of the Acropolis, which is Greek for "high city." The rock is 870 feet (265 m) long and 502 feet (153 m) wide, making it an ideal platform for the temples built there in the fifth century BCE.*

## The Erectheion

The Erectheion, another temple on the Acropolis, was named after Erectheus, a legendary king of Athens. It was built on the site of a mythical contest between Athena and the god of the sea, Poseidon. The temple contained an olive-wood statue of Athena (said to have dropped from heaven) that was reclothed every four years, during the Panathenaic festival. The Erectheion was famous for its south porch, which consisted of six columns carved as maidens, or caryatids.

Complementing these temples was the Propylaia, the formal gateway to the Acropolis, and the temple of Athene Nike (Athena as the goddess of victory), with its frieze depicting Greek victories, especially those against the Persians.

▼ *The Athenian sculptor Phidias showing visitors the frieze of the Parthenon, as depicted in a nineteenth-century painting by Lawrence Alma-Tadema. Phidias understood that because his art was public, he had to seek public approval. It is said he used to stand behind his studio door to listen to visitors' comments.*

**SEE ALSO**
• Athena • Athens
• Pericles

# Aeneid

The *Aeneid* is an epic poem in twelve books, composed by the Roman poet Virgil, to celebrate the origin and growth of the Roman Republic, the achievements of Rome, and its first emperor, Augustus. Virgil worked on the poem for ten years, funded throughout by Augustus. It was unfinished at the time of his death in 19 BCE.

## The Story

In the *Aeneid* the Roman people and their main families are glorified by stories of their ancestors. Rome is shown as a city blessed by the gods to rule, pacify, and civilize the world.

The hero of the poem is Aeneas, a refugee from the fall of Troy and the legendary founder of Rome. The *Aeneid* follows Aeneas on his journeys after the fall of Troy. He first visits Libya, where he falls in love with Dido, the queen of Carthage. However, despite Dido's love for him, he refuses to stay because he believes it is his destiny to go to Latium (Italy). Heartbroken, Dido kills herself.

Continuing his journey, Aeneas has many adventures and even visits the underworld – the place where Romans believed the spirits of the dead lived. Here Aeneas meets Dido's spirit and begs her forgiveness, but she turns away from him.

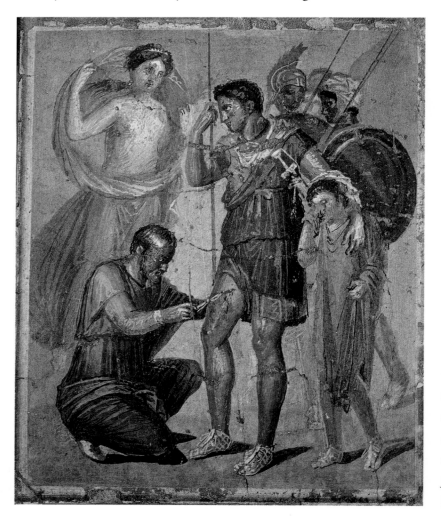

◀ A fresco from Pompeii showing Aeneas wounded in battle. The legend of Aeneas was taken very seriously by the Romans. Julius Caesar claimed to be his direct descendant.

A third-century-CE mosaic showing Virgil flanked by two of the muses. In Greek myth, the muses provided inspiration to artists. Here are shown Kilo (left), the muse of history, and Melomene, the muse of tragedy.

## VIRGIL 70–19 BCE

**Virgil (Publius Vergilius Maro) was born in Italy, near Mantua. After his education at Cremona and Milan, he came to Rome, where he met Maecenas, a patron of the arts and a personal friend of Augustus, who brought Virgil's work to the attention of the emperor. His main works are the *Eclogues*, a series of ten pastoral poems; the *Georgics*, a beautiful poem concerning agricultural techniques; and the *Aeneid*.**

**Virgil was still working on revisions to the *Aeneid* in 19 BCE when he was taken ill while traveling in Greece. He returned to Italy, where he died on September 20. He was buried near Naples. Before his death he requested that the *Aeneid* be destroyed because he had not finished revising the poem. However, Augustus believed that it was a work of great genius and commanded that it be published.**

**Virgil is regarded as one of the greatest poets of all time and has been studied and admired by schoolchildren and scholars from the Middle Ages to the present day.**

Finally Aeneas and his friends arrive in Latium and settle there.

## Importance

The *Aeneid* is arguably the greatest work of Latin literature to survive from the ancient world. It tells a great deal about the way the Romans thought, both about themselves and those they conquered, during the period of imperial expansion under Emperor Augustus. It is also a great poem in itself, with an exciting story and many beautiful passages. It has been quoted and admired by great writers throughout history, including the poets Chaucer, Tennyson, and Dante. Dante's admiration of the Aeneid and its author led him to make Virgil a major character in his own epic poem, *The Divine Comedy*.

### SEE ALSO

- Augustus • Carthage • Greek Mythology
- Roman Mythology
- Roman Republic and Empire
- Rome, City of • Troy

# Agamemnon

Agamemnon, son of Atreus, was the legendary ruler of the ancient Greek kingdom of Mycenae. In Homer's poem the *Iliad*, he commanded the Greek forces in the Trojan War. The war started when the Trojan prince Paris carried off Agamemnon's sister-in-law, Helen, who had been promised to Paris by the goddess of love, Aphrodite.

Archaeologists believe that the Trojan War was fought in about 1250 BCE. Agamemnon was probably a real king from that time. However, as most of what is known about him comes from the *Iliad* and from Greek plays of the fifth century BCE, there is uncertainty about the historical accuracy of the information from these sources.

## Commander of the Greeks

Agamemnon took one hundred ships to Troy – more than any other Greek king – so he was clearly wealthy and powerful. Homer portrayed him as a brave hero but not as a great leader. Twice Agamemnon became discouraged and wanted to give up on the war and go home. He had to be persuaded to stay by other heroes. On the

▶ This gold mask, which dates from around 1550 to 1500 BCE, comes from the royal tombs at Mycenae and is said to be the funeral mask of Agamemnon. It is now held at the National Archaeological Museum in Athens.

way to Troy, he sacrificed his own daughter Iphigeneia to the gods in return for fair winds for the Greek fleet. However, he nearly lost the war for the Greeks by offending the Greek champion Achilles.

This incident began when Agamemnon captured a Trojan woman to be his concubine. Her father was a priest of the god of sunlight and prophecy, Apollo, who forced Agamemnon to give her back. Annoyed by this order, Agamemnon arrogantly seized a woman whom Achilles had captured. Achilles was outraged, but Agamemnon refused to give her back. Insulted, Achilles left the battle for several days.

Nonetheless, as commander, Agamemnon won great glory when his forces eventually tricked their way into Troy by hiding in a huge wooden horse to gain entry and then destroying the city.

## Homecoming

Agamemnon arrived home with another concubine, the prophetess Cassandra. She predicted his death, but she was fated never to be believed. It had been ten years since Agamemnon had left home, and his wife, Clytemnestra, now had a lover, Aegisthus. Clytemnestra hated her husband for sacrificing their daughter Iphigeneia. Together Clytemnestra and Aegisthus stabbed Agamemnon to death. Different versions of this moment have been captured in Greek drama and art. For example, the playwright Aeschylus had Clytemnestra murder her husband by trapping him in a robe while he was in the bath and then stabbing him.

#### SEE ALSO

- Archaeology • Greek Mythology
- Iliad and Odyssey • Mycenaean Civilization
- Mythology • Troy

▲ This nineteenth-century painting depicts the scene when Clytemnestra, encouraged by her lover Aegisthus, goes to murder Agamemnon.

THE PLAYWRIGHT AESCHYLUS TELLS THE WHOLE STORY OF AGAMEMNON'S HOMECOMING AND MURDER AND HOW HE IS AVENGED EIGHT YEARS LATER BY HIS SON, ORESTES. THE STORY OCCUPIES THREE PLAYS, COLLECTIVELY KNOWN AS THE ORESTEIA. IN THE FOLLOWING PASSAGE FROM THE FIRST PLAY, AGAMEMNON, CLYTEMNESTRA TELLS HOW SHE KILLED HER HUSBAND.

*So that he could not escape or beat his death aside,*
*just as fishermen cast their enveloping nets, I spread*
*a deadly wealth of lavish robes, and trapped him fast.*
*I struck him twice. In two great cries of pain*
*he folded at the knees and fell. Once he was down*
*I dealt him the third blow, in thanks and praise*
*to Zeus the lord of dead men underground.*
*So he went down, and the life oozed out of him.*

# Agrippina

Agrippina the Younger (15–59 CE) was one of the most powerful women in ancient Rome. She was the wife of the emperor Claudius and mother of the emperor Nero. While Nero was a teenager, she effectively ruled Rome in his name.

Julia Agrippina was born in 15 CE. Her mother, Agrippina the Elder, was the granddaughter of Rome's first emperor, Augustus. Julia Agrippina's brother, Caligula, was emperor before Claudius. While Caligula was emperor, Agrippina led a very privileged life. Unlike most other women, she and her sisters were allowed to sit in special seats at the amphitheater; they also could own land and draw up legal documents and, in general, had much more freedom than ordinary women.

## From Exile to Empress

In late 39 CE Agrippina was accused of plotting against her brother, Caligula, who by now was exhibiting signs of madness. She was exiled from Rome to a small island until Caligula's death, after which she was pardoned by her uncle Claudius, the next emperor. When she returned to Rome, she was determined to achieve power and schemed to marry Claudius. He had a special law passed allowing him to marry his niece, and in 49 Agrippina became empress. She then persuaded her husband to adopt Nero, her son by an earlier marriage.

◄ A coin minted in 54 CE showing Agrippina on the left and the emperor Nero on the right. Agrippina's name and titles surround their heads. Nero's name and titles are on the other, less important side of the coin. This arrangement suggests that it was Agrippina who held the real power in Rome at this time.

Claudius died in 54 CE, probably as a result of being poisoned by Agrippina. Britannicus, his son by an earlier marriage and a possible rival to Nero, soon died, too, also poisoned. When he became emperor in 54, Nero was only sixteen years old, and so Agrippina effectively ruled in his place with the assistance of the great writer Seneca and the leader of the Praetorian Guard, Africanus Burrus.

## Agrippina's Death

As Nero grew older, he began to resent his mother's control over him. Finally, when she opposed his relationship with a woman of whom she disapproved, he had her sent away from Rome so that she could no longer interfere in his affairs. There followed several attempts by Nero to murder his mother – three times by poison, once by having the ceiling over her bed fixed to collapse on her, and once by trying to drown her in a collapsible boat. Finally he sent a murderer to Agrippina's house. In 59 Anicetus, a freed slave, went to her home and strangled and stabbed her to death.

Under a pretense of a reconciliation he [Nero] sent the most friendly note inviting her to celebrate the feast of Minerva with him at Baiae [a resort city sixteen miles west of Naples], and on her arrival made one of his captains stage an accidental collision with the galley in which she had sailed. Then he protracted the feast until a late hour, and when at last she said "I really must get back to Baiae," offered her his collapsible boat instead of the damaged galley. Nero was in a very happy mood as he led Agrippina down to the quay, and even kissed her breasts before she stepped aboard. He sat up all night anxiously waiting for news of her death. At dawn Lucius Agermus, her freedman, entered joyfully to report that although the ship had foundered, his mother had swum to safety, and he need have no fears on her account.

SUETONIUS, *THE TWELVE CAESARS*

### SEE ALSO

- Augustus • Caligula • Claudius • Nero
- Roman Republic and Empire

# Ahura Mazda

During their early history, around the seventh century BCE, the Persians worshiped many gods and spirits. By the time of the great Achaemenid kings (from 550 BCE), they worshiped one god, or supreme being, above all others. This god was Ahura Mazda, which means "wise lord." The Persians believed that Ahura Mazda inspired the prophet Zoroaster in a vision and instructed him in the rituals of worship.

Ahura Mazda was the force for good in the world. Everything good in life flowed from him. Persians even came to believe that Ahura Mazda had created the world and everything in it. However, Ahura Mazda was locked in an eternal struggle with his evil twin brother, Ahriman. Persians believed that Ahura Mazda needed the help of men and women in this fight to protect "justice" from an evil that they called "the lie." Followers of Ahura Mazda could win everlasting life after death if they helped the god by living good, pure lives.

The Persians did not build many temples, and they made no statues of their gods. They believed it was impossible – and bad luck – to show the shape of their god in human form. However, the image of a male figure with the wings and tail of an eagle, hovering in the air, is often found associated with an inscription involving the name Ahura Mazda. Some archaeologists believe that this may be a symbol for the supreme being.

## Persian Kings and Ahura Mazda

The Achaemenid kings usually allowed their subjects to worship their own gods. Xerxes himself worshiped the goddess Arta (whose name means "truth"). It seems that Ahura Mazda was mainly worshiped by the nobles at the royal court.

The great god and the king were very closely linked. Carvings of the figure in the

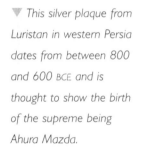

▼ This silver plaque from Luristan in western Persia dates from between 800 and 600 BCE and is thought to show the birth of the supreme being Ahura Mazda.

King Xerxes I (486–465 bce) ordered this inscription to be carved over the monumental gateway into the imperial palace at Persepolis:

*A great God is Ahura Mazda, who created this earth, who created yonder sky, who created man, who created happiness for man, who made Xerxes king, one king of many. . . . By the favor of Ahura Mazda, I built this Gateway of all Nations. . . . All beautiful things we have built, we have built by favor of Ahura Mazda. . . . May Ahura Mazda protect me and this land from harm. . . .*

▼ *Immense statues of creatures that were half man and half animal guarded the gateways into the royal palace of Persepolis. These led into the vast columned audience halls where the king met his subjects.*

winged disk, which may have been Ahura Mazda, have mostly been found at the royal palace at Persepolis guarding over images of the king carrying out his duties. According to inscriptions, the Persian kings believed that their power on earth was due to the protection of the god.

In the time of the later Sasanian kings, from the third to the seventh centuries CE, the Persians worshiped many gods, such as the sun god Mithra and the goddess of beauty, Anahita. However, Ahura Mazda was still the father of the gods.

## Sacrifice and Burial

Money was set aside by the kings to pay for sacrifices to the spirits of earth, wind, fire, and water. Worshipers of Ahura Mazda are said to have believed that burying or burning the bodies of the dead corrupted the earth and the air. Priests were therefore left exposed to the air and to wild birds and animals. Persian kings were covered in a layer of wax and then sealed within stone tombs. From the reign of Darius onwards, carvings of the figure in the winged disk watched over the dead rulers.

### SEE ALSO

• Achaemenids • Darius I • Persepolis
• Sasanians • Xerxes • Zoroastrianism

# Akkadians

The Akkadians are named after their city in central Mesopotamia, called Akkad (also spelled Akkade or Agade). The city has yet to be identified by archaeologists, but there are many references to it in written documents, and its existence is not doubted. In about 2340 BCE Sargon, the first Akkadian king, made Akkad the capital of his new state. Sargon ruled for over fifty years, and his successors maintained Akkadian supremacy for another hundred years.

## The World's First Empire

The reign of Sargon marked not only the beginning of Akkadian rule but also an important turning point in Mesopotamian history. The various Sumerian city-states were brought together under one ruler, and a new, more powerful state emerged in Mesopotamia.

During their period of dominance, the Akkadians created what has sometimes been called the world's first empire. They conquered Sumerian cities in southern Mesopotamia, such as Ur and Erech, and later, Akkadian power was extended farther, to the "four corners of the world," according to Mesopotamian texts recording the achievements of Akkadian kings.

Mesopotamian records claim that the Akkadians ruled from the Lower Sea (the present-day Persian Gulf) to as far west as the Upper Sea (the Mediterranean). Although there is very little evidence to support these claims, there is no doubt that the Akkadian state extended beyond Mesopotamia. However, evidence of an Akkadian presence does exist in what is now northern Syria, as well as in the land of the Elamites (now southwest Iran). The Akkadians traded through the Persian Gulf, but how far they established control over land to the east is not known.

▼ The land of Akkad in central Mesopotamia.

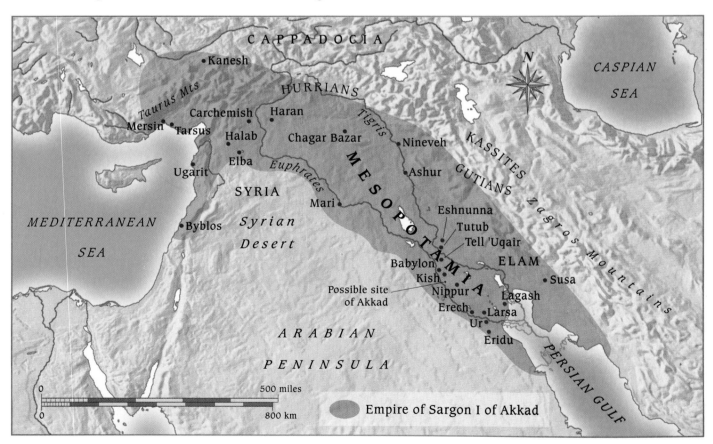

Empire of Sargon I of Akkad

## AKKADIANS

**2340 BCE**

Akkad is founded by Sargon.

**2284 BCE**

Death of Sargon.

**2260–2223 BCE**

Rule of Naram-Sin.

**c. 2150 BCE**

Akkad falls to attacks of mountain tribes.

◀ *Administrative matters, like the contracts recorded on these tablets from around 2300 BCE, gradually came to use Akkadian rather than the earlier Sumerian language.*

## Language

The Akkadians were a new force in the region, and they spoke their own language, quite different from the Sumerian language of the cities Ur and Erech. Royal inscriptions were first written in both the Sumerian and Akkadian languages, but over time Akkadian became the most widely spoken language of Mesopotamia.

The Akkadian language is the oldest-known member of the Semitic family of languages, a group of languages spoken in North Africa and Southwest Asia that includes Hebrew and Arabic. The Akkadian language developed two main dialects that continued to be used for a period of nearly two thousand years. The Assyrian dialect was used in northern Mesopotamia, and the Babylonian one spread outward from southern Mesopotamia to become, by the ninth century BCE, the more widely spoken and written language.

The Akkadian language has some six hundred signs for words and syllables, twenty consonants, and eight vowels and uses the present and the past tenses. The language was not deciphered until the nineteenth century CE, and in 1921 scholars at the University of Chicago began working on an Akkadian dictionary, of which twenty volumes have been published.

## Writing

The earliest Mesopotamian documents were written in Sumerian, a language that uses pictures both for objects and for the pronunciation of proper names. The use of lines in drawings gradually increased. Made by pressing the slanted edge of a reed stylus into soft tablets of clay, the lines have a wedge-shaped appearance. This style of writing is known by scholars as cuneiform, from the Latin word *cuneus*, which means "wedge." As cuneiform came to be adopted, the Akkadians began to write from left to right instead of in separate columns. The use of Akkadian written in the cuneiform script spread beyond Mesopotamia to other peoples, including the Elamites and the Persians.

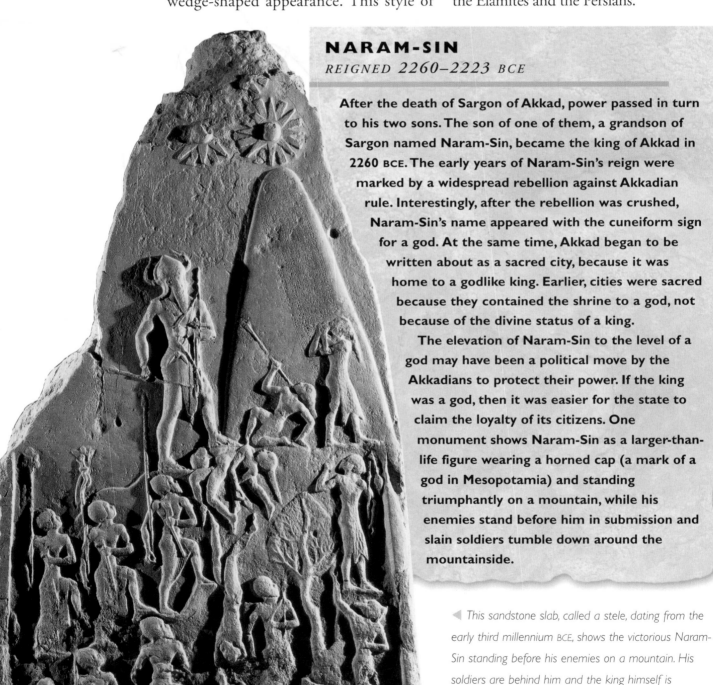

### NARAM-SIN
*REIGNED 2260–2223 BCE*

After the death of Sargon of Akkad, power passed in turn to his two sons. The son of one of them, a grandson of Sargon named Naram-Sin, became the king of Akkad in 2260 BCE. The early years of Naram-Sin's reign were marked by a widespread rebellion against Akkadian rule. Interestingly, after the rebellion was crushed, Naram-Sin's name appeared with the cuneiform sign for a god. At the same time, Akkad began to be written about as a sacred city, because it was home to a godlike king. Earlier, cities were sacred because they contained the shrine to a god, not because of the divine status of a king.

The elevation of Naram-Sin to the level of a god may have been a political move by the Akkadians to protect their power. If the king was a god, then it was easier for the state to claim the loyalty of its citizens. One monument shows Naram-Sin as a larger-than-life figure wearing a horned cap (a mark of a god in Mesopotamia) and standing triumphantly on a mountain, while his enemies stand before him in submission and slain soldiers tumble down around the mountainside.

◀ *This sandstone slab, called a stele, dating from the early third millennium BCE, shows the victorious Naram-Sin standing before his enemies on a mountain. His soldiers are behind him and the king himself is protected by the gods, whose symbols are at the top of the stele.*

Important works of literature, such as the Gilgamesh epic, were written in Akkadian and drew on earlier Sumerian sources. Archaeologists have uncovered thousands of clay tablets written in Akkadian, mostly dealing with such everyday matters as court decisions, marriage contracts, divorce settlements, and land sales.

## Kingship

The Akkadians developed the idea of kingship as a form of government. There were Sumerian kings before Sargon, but it was under the Akkadians that kings came to be seen as larger-than-life, spectacular figures.

The Akkadians showed the new importance they attached to kingship with the monuments they built. Large statues of kings were carved bearing inscriptions referring to the magnificence of royal power. This practice was very different from that of the Sumerians, who preferred to glorify their gods, not their rulers.

Arachaeologists have found two monumental Akkadian heads, one of stone and one of bronze. The bronze one, complete with a formal wig-helmet, may be a depiction of a king of Akkad, perhaps Sargon or Naram-Sin. The inscriptions on Akkadian monuments were a form of propaganda; sometimes several hundred lines in length, they highlighted the achievements of a king.

There is also a difference in style between the way the Sumerians and the Akkadians built their royal statues and monuments. The Akkadians, who liked to build on a grander scale than the Sumerians, left more space around the statue of the royal figure to emphasize his importance and made him larger in size than other figures.

▼ This bronze head of an Akkadian king, possibly Sargon, was found in the Temple of Ishtar in Nineveh. He is wearing a diadem and his beard looks as if it has been carefully cut and fashioned.

### The Curse of Akade

The new status of kings during the Akkadian period can also be seen in Mesopotamian literature from that time, which increasingly contained stories and myths about royalty. One such text is *The Curse of Akade*, thought to have been written some time after the collapse of the city of Akkad around 2150 BCE. Although this interesting text starts by describing the glories of Akkad, it goes on to describe a period of instability brought about by the chief god, Enlil (also known as Ellil), when he withdraws his favor from the city.

The Akkadian king becomes terribly depressed but finally rouses himself to challenge the god. He sets about attacking a temple to Enlil in another city, looting its riches and shipping them to Akkad. The god Enlil is enraged and seeks revenge by having Akkad attacked by an invasion of barbarians, who bring the life of the city to an end: "No one escapes their arms, messengers no longer travel the highways, boats no longer travel the rivers."

It is not possible to know for sure, but *The Curse of Akade* may reflect some of the tensions that arose in Akkadian society as individual kings became very powerful.

▼ *This is a modern impression made by an Akkadian cylinder seal showing a scene of a seated deity wearing a horned headdress, with an attendant and a bull supporting a winged gate. It dates from between 2300 and 2100 BCE.*

Such a situation could have led to conflict with temple priests fearful of too much power resting with one person. It is also possible that *The Curse of Akade* relates to a conflict between the older Sumerian rulers and the new Akkadian leaders. Before

Sargon, Sumerian kings ruled their own cities and local areas, but the Akkadians sought to unify different cities under one ruler and impose a central government.

## Military Power

The Akkadians probably maintained their military force for the purpose of keeping control over other cities. There was, for example, a need to crush rebellions by Sumerian cities after the death of King Sargon. It is possible that soldiers were recruited by promising them land taken from conquered territories. Monuments have been found that record the distribution of areas of land by an Akkadian king to his followers. One such monument also displays pictures of enemy soldiers being executed.

The Akkadian rulers extended their power by conducting military campaigns outside Sumer and establishing trade or exchange links with the people of other states. Money and goods were needed to pay the costs of administering such a large area. Money from trade or exchange or war booty was also needed to finance the army and the building of public monuments.

▲ *A fragment of an Akkadian victory stele showing two prisoners accompanied by a guard. The prisoners may well have ended up as slaves.*

## Decline

The Akkadian state gradually weakened, and around 2150 BCE the city of Akkad was attacked by mountainous tribes called the Amorites, a nomadic people from the northwest, and the Gutians, who came from the east. The city of Akkad survived the attack, but it never regained its powerful influence as the capital of southern Mesopotamia.

## Conclusion

The Akkadians changed the nature of Mesopotamian civilization by unifying the various Sumerian and Semitic cities under the rule of one powerful king. During Akkadian rule, literature and monumental architecture flourished. The popular legends of Akkadian kings lived on in written form long after the fall of the Akkadians, and they inspired neighboring cultures for generations to come. The concept of monarchy, government by a king, was developed to a new level by the Akkadians and became the dominant form of government in Mesopotamia for the next twenty-five hundred years.

▶ *This sculpture, dating from around the nineteenth century BCE, when the Akkadians had fallen to the Amorites, shows the goddess Ishtar with two priestesses on a mountain top.*

**SEE ALSO**

SOME IDEA OF THE PROSPERITY THAT AKKAD ENJOYED AS A RESULT OF FOREIGN CONTACTS MAY BE GLIMPSED FROM THIS DESCRIPTION OF THE CITY IN THE MESOPOTAMIAN TEXT *THE CURSE OF AKADE*. THE GODDESS ISHTAR HAS BLESSED THE CITY AND THE CONSEQUENCES ARE EAGERLY ANTICIPATED:

*So that the warehouses are provisioned,*
*that dwellings would be founded in the city,*
*that its people would eat splendid food,*
*that its people drink splendid beverages,*
*that those bathed would rejoice in the courtyards, that*
*the people would throng the places of celebration, that*
*acquaintances would dine together, that foreigners would*
*cruise about like unusual birds in the sky,*
*that monkeys, mighty elephants, water buffalo, exotic*
*animals, would jostle each other in the public square.*

# Alexander the Great

Alexander (356–323 BCE) was the son of King Philip II, ruler of Macedon, a mountainous country in northern Greece. Between 357 and 338 BCE, Philip had succeeded in conquering all the other Greek states. After Philip was murdered, Alexander became king. In just thirteen years, he enlarged the empire so that it stretched some three thousand miles (4,828 km), from Greece to India. This achievement earned him the title by which he has been known ever since – Alexander the Great.

### Early Life

Alexander's early education gave special emphasis to physical skills: sword fighting, riding bareback, athletics, and hunting. From thirteen he was taught for four years by the Athenian philosopher Aristotle, regarded as one of the wisest men of his time. Aristotle encouraged his pupil to be inquisitive about the natural world, an interest Alexander took with him on his later travels. Aristotle also taught him a love of literature. Though he was to become a great warrior, Alexander would also be a highly cultured monarch.

At the age of twelve, Alexander mastered an impossibly nervous horse because only he noticed that it was frightened by its own shadow. He named it Bucephalus and loved it dearly until its death. At sixteen, while Alexander was in charge of the kingdom in his father's absence, he put down a rebellion, leading the army himself.

Philip decided to marry a girl of about Alexander's age and make her his new queen in place of Olympias, Alexander's mother. At the wedding, a fight broke out between father and son, and Alexander and his mother left Macedon. Soon afterwards Philip was murdered, no one knows on whose orders, and Alexander was proclaimed king. He was twenty.

◀ This sculpture of Alexander the Great was created in the late second century BCE, possibly by the sculptor Menas. It is now in the Istanbul Archaeological Museum in Turkey.

▶ *A detail from the Alexander Sarcophagus, a marble chest with relief carvings of scenes from Alexander's life. The scene shown is from one of Alexander's battles. The sarcophagus was found at Sidon in modern-day Lebanon and was created around 300 BCE*

## Conquering the Persians

Alexander soon improved his father's already excellent army, brought the rebelling Greek states to heel, and then moved across the Hellespont into Asia Minor (now Turkey) to conquer Darius and the Persians. He would never set foot in Europe again.

He first met the Persian forces at the River Granicus. He was advised not to cross, as his men would have to struggle up the opposite bank under heavy attack. "But I should be ashamed of myself if a little trickle of water like this were too much for us," he replied, and then galloped ahead of his men to attack a Persian general. He broke his lance and nearly had his head cut off but was saved by one of his men, Cleitus. Alexander's army was victorious.

At Gordium he was shown an impossibly complex knot on the yoke of a cart and was told that the one who untied it would conquer Asia. Alexander, it is said, cut through it with his sword.

There followed more battles against armies, against cities, often against seemingly impossible odds. Alexander was as brave as any in battle, fearless and leading from the front. He was an inspiration to his men, and they adored him.

In victory he was often generous to the defeated and allowed them to live on and thrive. He continued to found new cities, usually named Alexandria, the most famous of which was and is in Egypt.

## India

In 327 BCE Alexander finally reached India. He won a few battles, but did not venture further east. He was halted not by an enemy but by his own army. His troops were unhappy being far from home and were disturbed by Alexander's preference for Persian ways in both his clothes and his behavior, as well as by his claim to be a god. Alexander had already killed his friend Cleitus for taunting him about his tastes.

## Death

The long march back began by a different route, and Alexander's army continued to conquer as it went. During an assault on one city, Alexander was seriously wounded. He and a large part of his army survived a terrible march through the Gedrosian Desert. In Babylon, the death of his best friend and companion, Hephaestion, deeply upset Alexander. Shortly afterward he caught a fever that became dangerous. As his death approached, he whispered that his kingdom should go "to the best" or perhaps "to the strongest." He was not yet thirty-three. Within a few years, his empire fell apart, his family all murdered. No one, it seems, was good enough or strong enough to hold it together.

## ROXANA

Roxana was Alexander's first wife and the only one, it is said, he married for love (he was to add two other wives later). She was the daughter of a warlord in Bactria (now Afghanistan), a country conquered by Alexander. She was said to be the most beautiful woman in the empire. Roxana was pregnant with Alexander's only son (the future Alexander IV) when he died. She then had another of his wives murdered and was later killed herself, as was her son, in the bloodshed that followed Alexander's death.

◄ This eighteenth-century painting depicts the engagement of Alexander and Roxana. Although he is said to have loved Roxana, Alexander also married her to strengthen his hold over Bactria.

### SEE ALSO

- Alexandria
- Aristotle
- Darius I
- Macedonians
- Philip II
- Warfare and Conquest

# Alexandria

When Alexander the Great reached Egypt in 332 BCE, he founded the city of Alexandria, twenty miles (32 km) west of the mouth of the Nile on the Mediterranean coast. After Alexander's death in 323 BCE, one of his generals, Ptolemy Soter, ruled Egypt. Ptolemy, his son Ptolemy II, and grandson Ptolemy III after him made the city famous. Alexandria became a great center for science, culture, and trade, with links to places as far away as China. Its lighthouse, which was around 445 feet (136 m) high with a lantern and mirror that made it visible for miles, became one of the Seven Wonders of the World.

## The Museum and Library

The lighthouse was Ptolemy Soter's idea, as was the idea for the building in which the lighthouse was designed – the Mouseion, or museum. Ptolemy wanted a library at Alexandria that would be bigger than the one at Athens. Ptolemy III wrote "to all the kings of the world," asking to borrow books for copying and translating. Even ships in the harbor, according to one story, were searched for books. Over time, about 700,000 manuscripts were collected.

## Research and Writing

Skilled scribes were needed for such work. The Ptolemies also invited scholars, scientists, and poets to do their research and writing at the Mouseion. As many as fifty might have worked there at any one time, paid for and housed by the royal family.

It was at the Mouseion in Alexandria, in the second century BCE, that Archimedes invented the threaded pump, known as the screw, to draw water from the Nile. The great mathematician Euclid wrote his

▶ A city plan of ancient Alexandria showing the positions of the lighthouse and the famous museum and library.

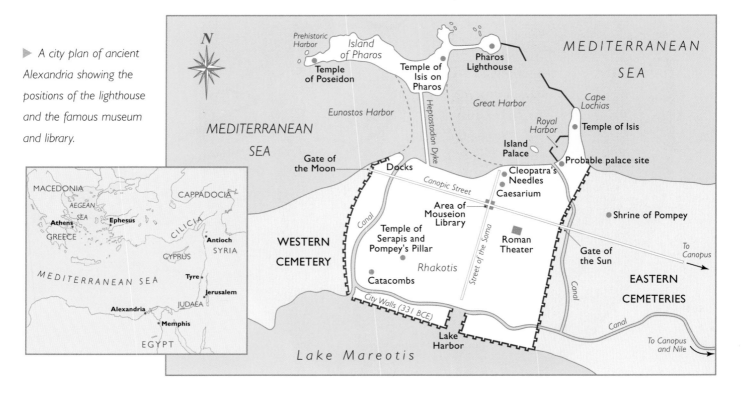

famous book *Elements* in Alexandria around 300 BCE. In 225 BCE the Alexandrian astronomer Eratosthenes calculated Earth's diameter at 7,850 miles (12,633 km), correct to half a percent. The poet Theocritus also worked there.

For a few hundred years, Alexandria was the scientific and cultural capital of the world. Then, in 48 BCE, much of the library burned down in a civil war.

## Pagans and Christians

Alexandria gradually declined in importance as a cultural center. In 30 BCE it became an occcupied city when the pharaoh Cleopatra was defeated by Octavian (the future emperor Augustus) and Egypt became part of the Roman Empire.

In 62 CE Christianity came to Alexandria. An early Christian named Saint Mark protested against the worship of Serapis and other traditional Egyptian gods, calling them "pagan" (nonbiblical) gods. Centers for Christian learning were set up, and the Christian population of Alexandria increased rapidly, even though it was persecuted by the Romans.

The fortunes of the Christians in Alexandria and elsewhere changed in 312 CE, when the Roman emperor, Constantine, converted to Christianity. The Coptic church (Egyptian Christians) became stronger, but trouble grew between Christians and pagans until 391, when the emperor Theodosius ordered the destruction of all pagan temples. In Alexandria the famous temple of Serapis and its library were destroyed.

### SEE ALSO

- Alexander the Great • Augustus
- Christianity • Cleopatra • Constantine

## HYPATIA *c. 370–415* CE

Contemporaries thought Hypatia was the finest philosopher of her time. An astronomer, philosopher, and mathematician, she was also a pagan at a time when Alexandria was becoming increasingly Christian. In addition, she was friendly with the local governor, Orestes, who had quarreled with the Christian bishop of Alexandria. In 415 CE Hypatia was attacked in the street by a group of Christian monks. They dragged her to a church, where they beat and cut her with *ostraka* (broken tiles) and burned her remains.

▼ *A nineteenth-century artist's impression of the library at Alexandria. The library was responsible for collecting and organizing the works of many Greek writers and poets. The librarians divided these into "books," corresponding to the standard length of a scroll.*

# Amaterasu

Amaterasu is the Japanese sun goddess. She is the most important deity in Shinto, the ancient Japanese religion that is still practiced. From early times Amaterasu was worshiped in southwest Honshu, the main Japanese island. From around 500 CE she was worshiped all over Japan.

## The Sun Goddess

According to legend, Amaterasu was the daughter of Izanagi, the creator god. He gave birth to her while washing his face after visiting the land of the dead. Soon afterward, Izanagi gave birth to two sons named Susano-wo and Tsuki-yomi. As she was his oldest child, Izanagi made Amaterasu the sun goddess and ruler of the heavens. Susano-wo became god of the oceans, and Tsuki-yomi became ruler of the night.

One of the main myths about Amaterasu tells how she quarreled with her brother Susano-wo after a miracle-working contest, which both deities claimed to have won. Susano-wo flew into a rage and frightened Amaterasu so much that she hid in a rocky cave. Without the sun goddess, day turned to night, and the world was plunged into everlasting, wintry darkness. Crops withered and died, so there was nothing for people to eat.

The other gods met and decided to lure Amaterasu from her cave. They gathered outside and made a lot of noise, but Amaterasu did not come out. Then the goddess Uzume began to dance. She became carried away and took off her clothes. The other gods started laughing. Amaterasu peeped out to find out what all the noise was about and was quickly hauled out of the cave. Thus, sunlight returned to light the earth.

▼ *This nineteenth-century painting by a Japanese artist shows the sun goddess Amaterasu emerging from the cave where she had previously been hiding from her brother.*

## Goddess of Farmers

After 500 CE most people in Japan worshiped Amaterasu, especially farmers, because sunlight was vital to ripen their crops. The main crop grown in Japan is rice, which is raised in flooded fields called paddies. Amaterasu was said to have taught humans how to grow rice and dig channels to flood the fields. In spring farmers prayed to Amaterasu as they planted the young rice shoots in the paddies. They asked her to grant a good harvest later in the year.

## The Yamato

Before about 300 CE Japan was not a united country. The islands of Japan were a patchwork of tiny states, each ruled by a powerful clan. Amaterasu was the main deity of a clan called the Yamato who ruled southwest Japan. Around 300 the Yamato gradually grew more powerful. Over the next two hundred years they conquered all of Japan and became the ruling dynasty. The Yamato have continued as emperors of Japan into the twenty-first century.

From early times Yamato chiefs claimed to be actually descended from Amaterasu. They also acted as high priests and as people who could pass on communications between the goddess and ordinary people. The rising sun, symbolizing Amaterasu, became the emperor's emblem and also the official symbol of the Japanese nation. A red circle representing the sun still appears on the Japanese flag.

▶ *Jimmu Tenno, the fabled first emperor of Japan, was said to be a direct descendent of Amaterasu. According to legend, Jimmu led an army eastward along Japan's Inland Sea, conquering tribes as he went, before establishing his empire in Yamato.*

### JIMMU TENNO

Jimmu Tenno was the legendary first emperor of Japan. According to myth he was a direct descendant of the god Ninigi, who was Amaterasu's grandson. Jimmu was said to have founded the Japanese empire in 660 BCE. In fact Japan did not become a unified nation until over a thousand years later, around 500 CE. According to legend Amaterasu gave Ninigi three gifts that became the symbols of the emperor's authority, a mirror, a sword, and some jewels. The gifts are believed to be still owned by Japan's ruling family.

**SEE ALSO**

• Japan

# Amenhotep III

Amenhotep III ruled Egypt from 1390 BCE to 1352 BCE. He was only a child when he became pharaoh, and his mother, Mutemwiya, appears to have ruled for him until he was old enough to rule alone. Egypt was at peace with her neighbors for most of his reign, so Amenhotep did not need to go to war. He simply made sure that the lands under Egypt's control sent regular payments, known as tribute, to Egypt.

Amenhotep III strengthened the bond between Egypt and several of its neighboring countries by marrying princesses from their ruling families. He maintained friendly relations with nearby rulers, such as Tushratta, king of Mittani, to the north of Egypt. Tushratta twice sent Amenhotep statuettes of his most important goddess to bless Amenhotep's two weddings to Mitannian princesses.

## Trade and New Ideas

Under Amenhotep Egyptians increasingly traded with other countries. He built a large new port at Thebes and moved the royal court from Memphis to Thebes. He also encouraged merchants, artists, craftsmen, and nobles from other countries to visit and live in Egypt.

Amenhotep expected the foreign peoples to learn Egyptian ways, but he was also interested in the new ideas these people might bring. Unlike most pharaohs, he introduced new ways of doing things. He ordered scribes to record the important events of his reign on scarab stones, which were large oval stones carved into the shape of the Egyptian scarab beetle. The flat undersides of these stones were inscribed with announcements of Amenhotep's marriages, building works, lion

◀ These giant sandstone statues, known as the Colossi of Memnon, are all that remain of Amenhotep's mortuary temple at Thebes.

hunts, and other events. The scribes made many copies of each scarab to send all over the kingdom and even abroad.

## Magnificent Buildings

Egypt was so peaceful and wealthy under Amenhotep III that he was able to spend a lot of time and wealth on building work. He ordered the construction of many temples and added to many more. He also made sure that his tomb and mortuary temples were ready in time for his death. Amenhotep III tried to limit the power of the priests of the god Amun. He tried to reduce their power by stressing the importance of other gods. He built many temples, large and small, to Ra in his role as the sun god, and to the Aten, another form of the sun god.

▶ *This statue of Amenhotep, son of Hapu, shows him as a scribe reading a scroll. Since scribes, as the only people who could read and write, administered Egypt for the pharaoh, being pictured in this way emphasized Amenhotep's learning and importance.*

## After Amenhotep

When Amenhotep died, his son Akhenaten (Amenhotep IV) moved the capital city to Amarna and changed Egypt's religion even further. He ordered people to worship only the sun god, the Aten. Akhenaten was a poor politician, and Egypt began to lose control of much of its foreign territory.

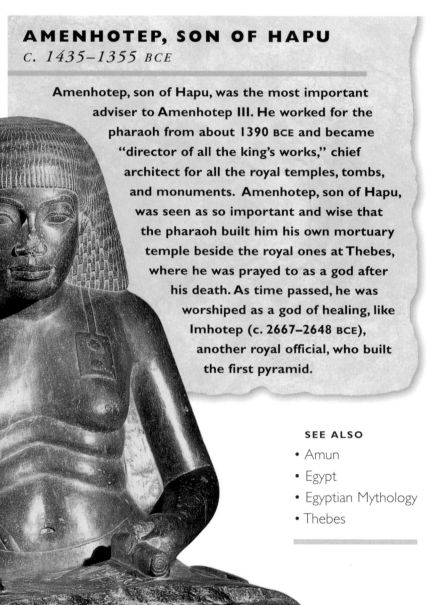

### AMENHOTEP, SON OF HAPU
#### c. 1435–1355 BCE

Amenhotep, son of Hapu, was the most important adviser to Amenhotep III. He worked for the pharaoh from about 1390 BCE and became "director of all the king's works," chief architect for all the royal temples, tombs, and monuments. Amenhotep, son of Hapu, was seen as so important and wise that the pharaoh built him his own mortuary temple beside the royal ones at Thebes, where he was prayed to as a god after his death. As time passed, he was worshiped as a god of healing, like Imhotep (c. 2667–2648 BCE), another royal official, who built the first pyramid.

### SEE ALSO

- Amun
- Egypt
- Egyptian Mythology
- Thebes

# Amun

The ancient Egyptians had many different gods and goddesses, each of which was responsible for a different area of life. The importance of individual gods and goddesses rose or fell, depending on who was ruling, because the pharaoh, who ruled the country, was also the head of Egypt's religion. From about 2000 BCE, under the pharaoh Mentuhotep II from the city of Thebes and the pharaohs who followed him, a god called Amun began to grow in importance.

## The First Worshipers

Amun was first worshiped in the area around Thebes. Most gods and goddesses were associated with particular animals and were shown in paintings with the head of one of these animals. The people of Thebes believed that the animals sacred to Amun were the ram and the goose. However, Amun was not shown in paintings and sculptures as a man with an animal's head. He was shown as a human wearing a headdress with two tall feathers on it.

## King of the Gods

In 1550 BCE Egypt, which had broken up into parts ruled by different minor pharaohs, was reunited by Ahmose I, a Theban pharaoh. Ahmose made Thebes his capital, and so the local gods of that city rose in importance. Amun's rise was rapid. By 1450 BCE Amun had been linked to the traditional sun god, Ra, and as Amun-Ra, was being described in temples and tombs as "king of all the gods." Pharaohs claimed to have been given their power by Amun.

## Different Forms

Over time Amun was linked to other gods, taking on their names and their power. As Amun Kematef he became the creator god, responsible for making things grow. As Amun came to be accepted as the most important god and the god that gave pharaohs their power, each pharaoh would enlarge Amun's great temple at Karnak.

The priests of Amun became very powerful. From about 1370 BCE the pharaoh Amenhotep III tried to limit the power of the priests, stressing the importance of other gods and goddesses, especially a different sun god, the Aten. For a short period, the Aten was made the only god of Egypt by Amenhotep's son, Akhenaten. When Akhenaten died, around 1336 BCE, his new religion was swept away, and the old gods, especially Amun, were worshiped again.

◀ These stone rams line the Avenue of the Rams at the Temple of Amun in Karnak. This part of the temple was built during the reign of the pharaoh Ramses II, who ruled from around 1279 to 1213 BCE.

When the Greeks under Alexander the Great conquered Egypt in 332 BCE, they worshiped Amun as Zeus-Ammon, joining Amun and Zeus, the most powerful Greek god. The Romans, who took over Egypt in 30 BCE, did the same, by joining Amun and Jupiter.

**SEE ALSO**

• Amenhotep III • Egypt • Egyptian Mythology • Thebes

PART OF A HYMN TO AMUN, WRITTEN IN ABOUT
1238 BCE:

*Amun will save those he loves, even if they
walk in the underworld
He will decide wisely, in his heart,
Who is worth saving.
Amun is all eyes, all ears as well
He guards all ways for those he loves.
He hears the cries of all who pray to him and
can come at once
To those who call him, no matter
how far away they are.
He can make a person's
life longer, or totally
disrupt it.
If he loves someone he
can shower him or
her with great riches.*

▶ *This statue of the god Amun was found in the Temple of Amun at Karnak. It was probably made during the rule of the pharaoh Tutankhamen who ruled from about 1336 to 1327 BCE. This was after the reign of Akhenaten when the Egyptians returned to worshiping many gods.*

# Analects

The *Analects* is a book of sayings by the Chinese philosopher Confucius, who lived from around 551 to 479 BCE. This famous book, prized and quoted all over China and other countries of eastern Asia, is also known as the *Lun Yu,* or *Conversations.*

## Confucius

Confucius was the most influential thinker of ancient China, yet no book exists that was definitely written by him. The philosopher spent much of his life working as a minor government official. When he retired, he became a wandering teacher who traveled around the various states of China offering advice on government to kings and rulers. Confucius was not well known in his lifetime. After his death his followers collected all his teachings and published them as a book: the *Analects.*

## The Teachings of the *Analects*

In Confucius's day Chinese society was generally lawless and chaotic, with many wars. The philosopher believed that things had been better in the past, and he called for a return to traditional values, including honesty and loyalty. He believed these values would allow society to become more peaceful and help people get along better. A famous passage from the *Analects* reads, "I want to reform society…. If we cannot live with our fellow men, with whom can we live? We cannot live with animals. If society was as it ought to be, I should not seek to change it."

Above all, Confucius stressed the importance of duty and obedience: of children to their parents and grandparents, of wives to their husbands, and of citizens to their rulers. As the *Analects* says, "A youth should be dutiful when at home, and abroad, respectful to his elders. He should

THE ANALECTS STRESSES THE IMPORTANCE OF LOYALTY, SINCERITY, AND THE TEACHINGS OF ANCIENT CHINESE PHILOSOPHERS. A MUCH-QUOTED PASSAGE FOLLOWS.

*Each day I examine myself on three points: whether I have been faithful in conducting business for others, whether I have been sincere in my dealings with friends, and whether I have mastered and practiced the instructions of my teacher.*

ANALECTS, CHAPTER 1, VERSE 8

servants who were educated along Confucian lines and who had a deep knowledge of the five books of Confucian learning. Confucianism was also enthusiastically supported by later Chinese dynasties. Confucius's ideas formed the basis of government in China for the next two thousand years.

SEE ALSO
• China • Chinese Philosophy
• Confucianism

be earnest and truthful. He should overflow with love for all and seek the friendship of the good."

The teachings of the *Analects* are broken up into chapters and verses. Some passages take the form of question-and-answer sessions between Confucius and his disciples. Other passages are just small pieces of wisdom, such as "Have no friends who are not equal to yourself" and "Do not be concerned about others not appreciating you. Be concerned about you not appreciating others." The people of ancient China learned these wise, witty words by heart.

## Confucianism Spreads

In the fourth and third centuries BCE Confucius's followers, including the philosophers Mencius (c. 390–305 BCE) and Xunzi (315–236 BCE), spread his ideas. Confucianism became increasingly popular after China became a unified empire in the 220s BCE.

During the reign of the Han emperors (202 BCE–220 CE), Confucianism became the official state philosophy. Under the Han dynasty, China was largely run by civil

▼ *This wood engraving shows Confucius with his disciples. It is from an edition of the* Analects *made during the Ming Dynasty (1368–1644 CE).*

# Anasazi

The Anasazi were prehistoric people who lived in the southwestern part of the United States on the Colorado Basin and the San Juan plateau. Local people call this area the Four Corners, the point where modern-day New Mexico, Arizona, Colorado and Utah meet.

The Anasazi were pueblo people, that is, they lived in villages. Anasazi villages included homes built out of stone and sun-dried brick. The name Anasazi means "the ancient ones" in the Navajo language. Navajo and Hopi are the names given to the Native Americans who live in this part of the United States. The Navajo language is still spoken there by people who are probably descendants of the Anasazi. The major period of Anasazi culture began around 200 CE. The Anasazi of that time were known as Basket Maker people.

## Houses

The first Basket Maker people were farmers and hunters, and they lived in the Rio Grande valley in Nevada from about 1 CE. They formed small village communities, usually comprising a few oval or circular pit houses dug into and built below the surface of the ground. A doorway in the ceiling opened from the ground above, and people went down into the house by way of a ladder.

The underground house helped protect people from the hot sun during summer and kept them warm in the winter. As populations grew, buildings began to be constructed above ground; they were used as places both to live and to store food. These structures later developed into pueblos, forming a D shape on several levels. Surviving examples can be seen at places like Pueblo Bonito and Mesa Verde.

## Religion and Worship

The earliest Anasazi people also built ceremonial rooms known as kivas. Like the pit houses, they too were built below ground, and they symbolized the underworld from which people are supposed to have emerged to live on earth. The Hopi origin myth describes how these people were led through a doorway in the sky to the upper world. The walls in these kivas were decorated with colored painted murals.

▼ *The territories of the Anasazi, Hohokam, and Mogollon peoples of the southwest of North America.*

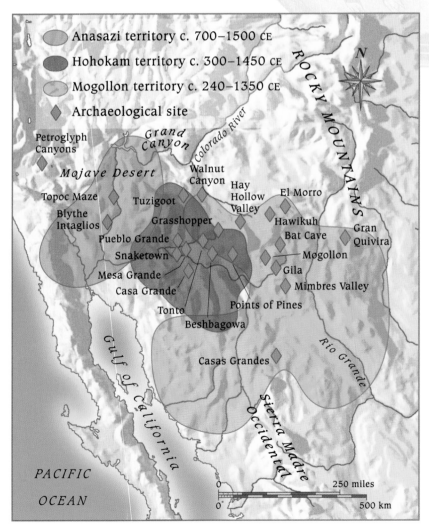

Anasazi territory c. 700–1500 CE
Hohokam territory c. 300–1450 CE
Mogollon territory c. 240–1350 CE
◆ Archaeological site

ROCKY MOUNTAINS
N

Colorado River
Grand Canyon
Petroglyph Canyons
Mojave Desert
Walnut Canyon
Hay Hollow Valley
El Morro
Topoc Maze
Tuzigoot
Blythe Intaglios
Grasshopper
Hawikuh
Gran Quivira
Pueblo Grande
Bat Cave
Snaketown
Mogollon
Mesa Grande
Gila
Casa Grande
Mimbres Valley
Points of Pines
Tonto
Beshbagowa
Casas Grandes
Rio Grande
Gulf of California
Sierra Madre Occidental
PACIFIC OCEAN

0    250 miles
0    500 km

## ANASAZI

**c. 1 CE**

First signs of the Anasazi people in the Four Corners region.

**c. 200 CE**

First evidence of the Basket Maker culture.

**c. 400 CE**

First evidence of the Mogollon and Hohokam cultures.

**c. 500 CE**

Culture flourishes; major building works are undertaken.

**c. 700–1050 CE**

Pueblo I and Pueblo II periods.

**c. 1050–1300 CE**

Classic pueblo period (Pueblo III); building of Chaco Canyon and Mesa Verde.

*In the beginning, there was only Tokpella, Endless Space . . . only Tawa, the Sun Spirit, existed, along with some lesser gods. There were no people then, merely insectlike creatures who lived in a dark cave deep in the earth.*

*Tawa led the creatures through two levels of the world. Eventually, they climbed up a bamboo stalk through the sipapuni, the doorway in the sky, into the Upper World. There the gods gave them corn and told them to place a small sipapuni in the floor of each kiva.*

HOPI ORIGIN MYTH (RETOLD BY BRIAN M. FAGAN IN *KINGDOMS OF GOLD, KINGDOMS OF JADE*).

## Farming and Hunting

The Anasazi were skilled at making use of what little rain fell to irrigate their crops. However, the climate in the area where they lived, with its fiercely hot summers and bitterly cold winters, made growing crops very difficult.

▲ The site of the Anasazi settlement at Chaco Canyon, in New Mexico. This was the center of the Anasazi civilization from the ninth century to about 1300 CE. The circular pits were probably cellars used for storage.

## THE MOGOLLON AND HOHOKAM PEOPLES

*This Mogollon pottery bowl, painted in the Mimbres style, shows two figures. They may represent the contest between male and female or between life and death. Such bowls were placed as burial offerings with holes punched in the bottom to help release the vessel's spirit into the next world.*

Other people lived in the region near the Anasazi. The Mogollon were highland farmers who lived in what is now part of New Mexico and Arizona. Among the Mogollon people was a group called the Mimbres, whose female potters made pottery bowls formed from long strips of clay wound into coils, fired, and then painted with elaborate designs, including insects, sheep, bats, birds with outstretched wings, and a man spearing fish.

The bowls were not made just for decoration. When a person died, his or her relatives would place some bowls in the grave with the body, having first punched a hole in the bottom of each bowl. Scholars believe the hole was made to free the spirit of the painted creature or figure. Mogollon people were also stonemasons, and they made ornaments from copper bells imported from Mexico.

The Hohokam lived on the banks of the Gila River, which was a fertile strip in the middle of hot desert country. Like the Anasazi, they dug irrigation channels to water their crops. Archaeologists have discovered a Hohokam settlement known as Snaketown (the Native American name Shoaquik means "place of snakes"), which was originally made up of pit houses and dwellings made of poles covered in brushwood. Ball courts have also been discovered that are similar to but smaller than the famous ones built by the Maya and the Olmecs.

*The dwellings and kivas in the Cliff Palace at Mesa Verde. The kivas are the circular shapes in the foreground of the picture. The settlement was lived in by the Basketmaker and Pueblo Indians around the twelfth century CE.*

Historians believe that the climate played an important part in the way small communities formed and then frequently disappeared. People moved on if crops failed, and settlements from these earliest days are hard to trace. Most evidence also suggests that the Anasazi did not depend solely on farming for their survival; they were also skilled at hunting animals and catching fish.

## Decorative Art

The baskets made by the Basket Maker people were made from coiled strips of willow, wound around and then sealed and made watertight with the gum of the pinon tree. They were decorated with red, black, and white geometric patterns. Later, the Anasazi made pots and other ceramic vessels. These too were painted with symbolic figures in black and red.

## What Happened to the Anasazi?

The next periods in Anasazi development, known as Pueblo I and Pueblo II, lasted roughly from 700 to 1050 CE. The people of this time built larger villages of houses with rooms above ground, often connected to each other and built around a dance plaza. The classic Pueblo period (c. 1050–1300 CE), saw the building of the most famous surviving sites, those at Mesa Verde and Chaco Canyon. At Pueblo Bonito and Chaco Canyon and in the surrounding villages, up to six thousand people are believed to have lived; daily life included trading, ritual worship, and celebration.

From 1150 CE the Anasazi moved to other areas, such as the Mesa Verde. There is evidence that Chaco Canyon was suddenly deserted, and the reason may have been a drought that began in 1130. The Anasazi maintained their political, social, and ritual way of life, based on the word of leaders believed to have been guided by the gods. By the time the Europeans arrived in 1530, pueblo people were widely scattered in smaller groups but retained a common culture.

**SEE ALSO**
• Hopewell Culture • Maya

# Angles and Saxons

The Angles and the Saxons invaded Britain from the area of present-day Denmark and northern Germany in the middle of the fifth century CE. By 600 the culture and language of the Angles and Saxons dominated a large part of Britain. That region came to be called England, a name that is a modern version of "Angle land."

### The End of Roman Britain

In 410 CE the Roman emperor Constantine III, as a result of civil war and barbarian invasions, wrote to the cities of Britain, asking them to organize their own defense.

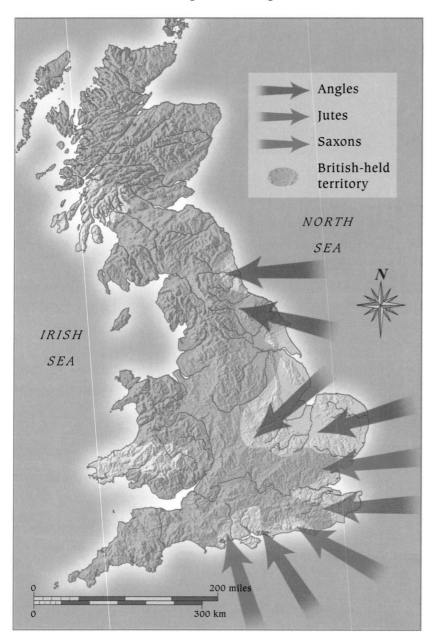

▼ A map of Britain, showing the invasions and territorial possessions of the Angle, Saxon, and Jute raiders by 500 CE.

Angles
Jutes
Saxons
British-held territory

*NORTH SEA*

*IRISH SEA*

N

0        200 miles

0        300 km

Thus ended the Roman rule of Britain. The people of Britain were being attacked by Irish, Pictish, and Anglo-Saxon raiders. The only contemporary source, written by a man named Gildas, indicates that a great council was held to discuss the crisis. The Britons decided to hire Saxon mercenaries to protect them.

### Guests Become Invaders

Trouble arose when the Britons stopped providing the Saxon soldiers with the supplies they needed. In about 450 the Saxons rebelled and began attacking the Britons. The Saxons were soon joined by Angles, Jutes, and Frisians, also from northern Europe. These tribes were closely related, and their languages were very similar.

### War

War was a way of life for the Germanic tribes. Many of the early English poems and songs tell stories of heroic battles. The Angles and Saxons fought on foot and were very lightly armed. Only the richest soldiers had helmets and swords. Most warriors used wooden shields and spears with iron tips.

Each warrior chief had a group of companions. If a chief was killed in battle, his companions had to continue fighting to the death. If they left the battlefield alive, they would be disgraced for the rest of their lives. The powerful bond between a chief and his companions was called allegiance.

**ANGLES AND SAXONS**

| **410 CE** | **c. 440 CE** | **c. 450 CE** | **c. 500 CE** |
|---|---|---|---|
| Roman rule ends in Britain. | Some Saxons are invited to help defend Britain. | The Saxons rebel against the British. They are joined by Angles, Frisians, and Jutes. | The Britons defeat the Saxons at Badon Hill. |

## The Battle of Badon Hill

During the second half of the fifth century CE, as more invaders arrived, some Britons fled across the sea to northern France, to an area that became known as Brittany. In about 500 a great battle was fought at a place called Badon Hill, somewhere in southwest England. The Britons won a famous victory, and the two sides agreed to a truce. In spite of this setback, the Anglo-Saxons continued to expand their territory. It was not until 1066 and the victories of William the Conqueror at Hastings and elsewhere that the Anglo-Saxon kingdom came to an end. Although people in Wales and Brittany still speak Celtic languages, it is the language of the Angles and Saxons – English – that dominates Britain.

# RELIGION

The most famous gods of the Germanic invaders were Tir, Woden, Thor, and Frija. In English four days of the week are named after them: Tuesday, Wednesday, Thursday, and Friday, respectively. The word Easter derives from Eostre, the goddess of spring, whose symbols were a hare and an egg.

The religion of the Angles and Saxons was based on the natural world, and they worshiped in forests and at lakes. They buried human sacrifices to their gods in peat bogs. Archaeologists have found well-preserved bodies in peat bogs in the Anglo-Saxon homelands of Denmark and Germany.

◀ This Anglo-Saxon bowl was found in Kent and dates from about 600 CE. It is made of glass with a trailed decoration looping around it.

**SEE ALSO**

• Celts • Franks • Roman Republic and Empire

# Antony, Mark

Mark Antony (c. 83–30 BCE) was one of the most important figures in the final years of the Roman Republic. A politician and a soldier, he tried to become the sole ruler of the Roman world.

### Antony and Julius Caesar

Antony's career began in the army. Between about 58 and 56 BCE he campaigned in Egypt as a cavalry commander. In 54 BCE he was in Gaul (present-day France and Belgium) serving with Julius Caesar. Two years later Antony entered the Roman senate. His loyalty to Caesar showed itself in 49 BCE, when his friend tried to become consul. The senate ordered Caesar to disband his troops or be declared an enemy of Rome. Antony spoke in Caesar's defense and was expelled from the senate. In the civil war that followed, Antony led part of Caesar's army. Caesar was triumphant.

▼ A portrait of Mark Antony on a gold coin, struck around 41 BCE, after he had become one of the three rulers of the Roman world.

### Struggle for Power

Caesar rewarded Antony by making him his coconsul. When Caesar was assassinated in 44 BCE, Antony was left with almost total power, and he called for support from the army and the people. However, Caesar had named his adopted son, Octavian (who later became Augustus), as his heir, not Antony. The two men, who had been allies, now became rivals. In 43 BCE at Mutina (present-day Modena in Italy), Antony was defeated by Octavian's forces. Antony retreated to Gaul, where he allied himself with the general Marcus Aemilius Lepidus. Fearing another civil war, Octavian made peace with Antony and Lepidus. The three men, in an alliance known as the Second Triumvirate, shared control of the Roman world. In 42 BCE Octavian and Antony's forces defeated the last of Caesar's assassins in two battles at Philippi in Greece. Antony went on a triumphal tour through Greece and the East, and in 41 BCE he met Cleopatra, the pharaoh of Egypt.

### Antony and Cleopatra

Antony was captivated by Cleopatra, and despite being married to Octavian's sister, he fell in love with her. He briefly stayed with Cleopatra in the Egyptian city of Alexandria. In 36 BCE Antony led an unsuccessful war against Parthia, a region in the east. This defeat, along with his interest in the affairs of Egypt at the expense of Rome's, caused his downfall. The senate

▲ A nineteenth-century painting of Mark Antony making his famous speech in the Roman forum at the funeral of Julius Caesar in 44 BCE.

stripped Antony of his powers and declared war on Cleopatra.

In 31 BCE a sea battle was fought near Actium, off the west coast of Greece, between Antony's and Octavian's fleets. Antony lost the battle and returned to Alexandria with Cleopatra. The following year, before Octavian's forces entered the city, Antony and Cleopatra killed themselves. Antony's death cleared the way for Octavian's rise to power and the start of the Roman Empire.

**SEE ALSO**

HERE IS AN ACCOUNT OF MARK ANTONY'S SPEECH AT CAESAR'S FUNERAL, ACCORDING TO THE GREEK HISTORIAN PLUTARCH (C. 46–C. 120 CE):

*As Caesar's body was carried out for burial, Antony gave the funeral speech in the Forum. When he saw that his words had cast a spell over the people there, and that they were affected by what he had said, he spoke of the horror at what had happened [that Caesar had been murdered]. As he was ending his speech, he snatched up Caesar's robe and held it up, showing the people the stains of blood and the holes of the many stabs, and calling those that had done this act villains and murderers.*

PLUTARCH, *LIVES: MARK ANTONY*

# Aqueducts

Aqueducts are stone channels raised on walls, columns, or arches in order to carry water across a valley. The first aqueduct in the world was built in Assyria during the seventh century BCE.

### Sennacherib's Aqueduct

Around 691 BCE the Assyrian king Sennacherib ordered the construction of a ten-mile (16 km) long water channel. The channel fed water from eighteen different sources in the nearby mountains into Nineveh, Sennacherib's capital city. Where the water supply had to cross a valley the Assyrians raised the water channel on five stone arches and thus created the first aqueduct.

Some nine hundred yards (823 m) long, the aqueduct was made from hardened earth and was waterproofed with molten tar. The arches were thirty feet (9 m) high in places. The canal was fed by small streams to ensure that Nineveh had enough water for its parks, palaces, and botanical gardens. Two small dams controlled the flow of fresh water.

Sennacherib's famous aqueduct was destroyed in 612 BCE, when Nineveh was sacked by the Babylonians and the Medes. Its ruins, however, inspired the ancient Romans to build a series of aqueducts that were the envy of the world.

▶ This stone relief, carved in the late seventh century BCE, shows King Sennacherib of Nineveh overseeing workers in a quarry. They are extracting stone for the building of the king's famous aqueduct.

## Roman Aqueducts

At the beginning of the fourth century CE, the city of Rome required a total of about 38 million gallons of fresh water piped in every day. To satisfy this need, between 312 BCE and 226 CE the Romans built eleven aqueducts to bring water from the surrounding hills to their city.

Most of the Roman aqueducts were built of limestone. In places where the water channels passed high above the ground, they were supported by up to three rows of arches built on top of each other. Others aqueducts consisted of underground pipes made of stone, clay, wood, and bronze.

Channels and pipes were sloped to allow water to flow freely through the aqueduct. Water was collected in special tanks called *castella* within the city precincts before it was channeled out to public baths and the wealthier private houses. Extra water was used to flush out the city's sewers.

The water channels at the top of the open-air aqueducts were usually three feet (91 cm) wide and six feet (183 cm) high. This design made it possible for workers to walk along the aqueducts and deal with any cracks or blockages. A team of repairmen worked constantly under the supervision of a curator to keep the aqueducts in excellent condition. Underground pipes could be inspected through airshafts dug into the hills.

## Decline and Destruction

The Romans built aqueducts all over their empire, including North Africa and in countries like France, Spain, Greece, Italy, and Malta. As the empire began to decline in the fourth century CE, many of the aqueducts fell into disrepair. In the fifth century CE, the Ostrogoth warlord Vitiges

had ten of Rome's aqueducts destroyed and thereby cut off most of the city's water supply. He missed one, however, known as the Aqua Virgo, because it ran mostly underground. In time this aqueduct also fell to ruin as people went back to fetching water from rivers and wells.

> The rent that is collected from private individuals who are supplied with water may be applied by collectors to the maintenance of the aqueduct.
>
> ROMAN ARCHITECT MARCUS VITRUVIUS POLLIO, DE ARCHITECTURA, BOOK 8

▲ This triple-tiered Roman aqueduct was built around 19 BCE in Gard valley outside Nîmes in France. It is some 160 feet (49 m) high. The lower level was also a bridge, strong enough to take the weight of men and chariots. The upper level carried water to Nîmes from a spring 31 miles (50 km) to the north.

**SEE ALSO**

- Architecture • Assyrians • Rome, City of
- Sennacherib

# Archaeology

Archaeology is the study of humankind's past through investigation of its artifacts. The past is a jigsaw puzzle that tells the whole story of humankind. To make sense of the past, archaeologists have to learn how to join the pieces together, and they have developed many different techniques to accomplish this task.

## Making Sense of the Past

During the 1700s and early 1800s CE, people became increasingly curious about the distant past. At that time European collectors called antiquarians began to search for ancient artifacts buried in the ground. They knew that the things they found were old, but they had no way of knowing how old. Museums in Europe amassed collections of curiosities – stone tools, pots, metalwork – all unearthed by antiquarians. Display cases filled up with a clutter of ancient objects, but there was little or no attempt made to put them into any kind of order.

◀ The interior of a London museum in the 1780s, showing how ancient objects were brought together to be admired. Rooms like this were often disorganized, cluttered places.

# EXCAVATING A SITE

Excavation is the main technique used to uncover the secrets of an archeological site. It is the process of physically digging into the site layer by layer. Archaeologists call these layers the site's "stratigraphy." They work backward through time, starting at the top of the site, where the recent layers are, and stopping only when they reach the geological layer at the very bottom, where there are no traces of human activity. It can be slow work since the soil is usually scraped away with small hand trowels and carried off the site in buckets and wheelbarrows.

In a modern excavation, data are carefully and accurately recorded so they can be studied after the excavation ends. Plans are drawn to show the positions of walls, ditches, pits, and other features. The positions of objects — potsherds, bones, and flints, for example — are all recorded. After the site has been excavated, a team of archaeologists studies its data. The team is able to determine how old the site is, what happened there through time, and how and when its history came to an end. A detailed report is published describing what was found and what has been learned about the site.

Archaeology is a destructive science, since excavation disturbs and removes buried deposits. In this respect archaeology differs from other branches of science. Laboratory-based experiments can often be repeated over and over again, but archaeologists only ever have one chance to dig a site. Thus, data recording is very important, since a site's data are a record of its existence.

▲ A nineteenth-century archaeologist makes notes at the site of Troy's ruins in Hissarlik, Turkey. The site was first excavated by the German archaeologist Heinrich Schliemann during the 1870s.

▲ Archaeologists use small tools to carefully remove soil from around the skull of a human skeleton. After photographing, it will be lifted and taken away to be studied.

## The Three Age System

In 1817 Christian Thomsen (1788–1865), the curator of the National Museum of Denmark, attempted to make sense of the objects in his care. He sorted all the cutting tools into three groups, depending on whether they were made from stone, bronze, or iron. His classification was called the Three Age System – Stone Age, Bronze Age, and Iron Age. It was a very simple and effective time line. Thomsen's breakthrough was soon confirmed by fieldwork – objects from the oldest period, the Stone Age, lay beneath ones from the Bronze Age, which in turn were underneath ones from the Iron Age. The Three Age System was put to use in dating artifacts and is still employed.

## Modern Archaeological Techniques

In addition to excavation, archaeologists now use many other techniques to study the past. At certain times of the year, archaeological features buried below ground level can be seen from the air and photographed for later study. They show up as patterns of light or dark marks in fields and are termed crop marks. By walking across the same field after it has been plowed, field walkers look for objects turned up by the plow. The objects will help archaeologists determine what type of site lies under the field. A geophysical survey might then take place, using machines that can "see" below ground level. Sensors are used to detect buried walls, pits, and ditches, without the need to dig into the site.

*Flinders Petrie, the father of modern archaeology, photographed around 1885.*

## SIR WILLIAM MATTHEW FLINDERS PETRIE *1853–1942*

Few people have influenced the development of modern archaeology as much as Flinders Petrie. Born in Kent in England, he was interested in old things from an early age. In his twenties Petrie surveyed prehistoric stone circles in southern Britain.

In 1880 Petrie went to Egypt to measure the Great Pyramid at Giza. He devoted almost the rest of his life to the study of ancient Egyptian language, culture, objects, and archaeology. Petrie excavated many of Egypt's major sites, where he used scientific techniques to record what he found. Rather than throw away ordinary objects and shards of pottery as other archaeologists did, Petrie kept and recorded everything so that others could study the evidence.

Petrie developed a dating system known as sequence dating in which he grouped pottery and other objects into families. Petrie's method enabled archaeologists to date their sites on the basis of the way in which objects changed their appearance over time. His work led to a better understanding of the past, and through his students and books, his methods were spread worldwide.

During and after an excavation, samples of organic material (wood, leather, and bone, for example) might be sent away to be dated using radiocarbon analysis. This is a special technique that is used to date objects up to about 50,000 years old. Older objects, up to about 100,000 years old, can be dated using potassium argon dating. A more accurate dating technique is dendrochronology, which uses tree rings to fix the age of a piece of timber to an exact year (the year in which the tree was felled) by comparing it with the rings from trees whose ages are known. Dendrochronology can be used to date wooden objects that are up to about five thousand years old.

Another type of laboratory-based archaeology is environmental archaeology, where pollen grains and seeds are recovered from soil samples. By identifying them, it is possible to work out what plants grew in the ancient landscape and which ones were cultivated by farmers.

There is also another approach, known as experimental archaeology, in which archaeologists use the materials and methods of the past to make things such as buildings, pots, stone and metal tools, textiles, and other objects. By re-creating them as authentically as possible, archaeologists are able to understand the processes used by people of the past. It is a case of learning through experiment.

**SEE ALSO**

- Cities • Mummification • Pottery
- Pyramids • Tombs

# Architecture

Civilization breeds architecture. Wandering peoples made do with tents and other temporary structures. When people began to settle in one place, to grow crops and make tools, handicrafts and artworks, they also started building. They constructed houses, workshops, meeting places, storage places, shrines, and temples for their gods.

Civilizations developed in regions where buildings were fairly easy to construct, using local materials. In hot countries, such as Egypt and India, they built with dried mud bricks, with pebble and straw mixed in for added strength. In cooler regions, such as northern Europe, they built with clay, mud, wicker, wood, and stone.

## Houses

Climate affected the design of early houses. Egyptian houses had small windows to keep the interiors cool. In the settlement of Skara Brae in Orkney, off the north coast of Scotland, the endless winds forced the inhabitants to build into the ground for shelter. Even in such harsh surroundings, the people of Skara Brae tried to make their half-buried homes comfortable with shelves, alcoves, cupboards, and beds, all built from stone.

In the Indus valley, between about 2500 and 2000 BCE, many of the larger houses in the cities of Mohenjo Daro and Harappa had two stories, with several rooms arranged around an open courtyard. Larger Egyptian houses also had touches of luxury: their inside walls were painted with designs or scenes from nature.

## Walls

Towns needed to be defended, usually by walls. Walls were built all over the world. The Chinese had walled towns by about 2500 BCE. In Mesopotamian Ur, around 2100 BCE, the defenses were a massive sloping rampart of mud brick, with walls above. Archaeologists who discovered parts of the ruined walls of the city of Jericho (in present-day Palestine) date them to about 7000 BCE.

## Pyramids and Temples

Early civilizations expressed their religious feeling and beliefs through the structures they built, especially mounds and pyramids. The Chinese built pyramids from about 3000 BCE, while the Egyptians built their first pyramids around 2650 BCE. In Mespotamia the pyramid mound was

▼ In ancient Harappa, Pakistan, these ruined walls of dried mud brick, built between 2500 and 2000 BCE, are what remains of a neighborhood of craftsmen's workshops.

called a ziggurat; it consisted of a series of ascending mud brick terraces decorated with mosaics and planted with trees. It was a structure dedicated to the god of the city, with a temple at the top.

At about the same time, around 2600 BCE, mounds with templelike structures were being built on the central coast of Peru. Later, Mesoamericans began to build a kind of pyramid temple – a steep, four-sided pyramid with stairs on one side and a broad, flat summit with a temple. A famous example is the great Zapotec temple at Monte Albán called Temple of the Dancers, dating from about 500 BCE.

## City Planning

Developments in architecture caused city life to grow more comfortable. Indus valley cities, such as Mohenjo Daro and Harappa, had houses with sewers, private wells, and private baths. Public baths became common in the towns and cities of the Roman Empire two thousand years later. Rome's excellent sewage sytems and aqueducts laid the basis for healthy living.

Cities were sometimes planned. Teotihuacán in Mesoamerica, with about 45,000 inhabitants by 100 CE, was laid out carefully in a grid pattern, as were the cities of Mohenjo Daro and Harappa in India.

*▲ An eighteenth-century engraving of the interior of the Pantheon in Rome, built in the second century CE by the emperor Hadrian. It was built of brick with a great hemispherical dome. The illustration shows the interior of the temple and the covered walkway, or portico, leading to the entrance.*

The design of Çatal Hüyük in central Anatolia, where perhaps six thousand people lived in about 7000 BCE, was quite different. Its houses of mud brick and plaster were all linked to each other like cells in a beehive – it was a city with no streets. To get to their houses, people climbed down ladders from flat rooftops.

## New Ideas

The Greeks developed new architecture to meet the needs of their new ideas. Their democratic ways demanded spaces for meeting and talking, such as the agora, or marketplace, the colonnaded way, the council chamber. Their athletics inspired the gymnasium and the stadium. From about 600 BCE they built great stone amphitheaters for performing their plays.

# THE TUNNEL OF EUPALINOS ON SAMOS

*On the Greek island of Samos, a tunnel 1400 yards (1280 m) long and eight feet (2.4 m) wide was built through a mountain to bring water to the city. The tunnel was the work of a sixth-century-BCE engineer named Eupalinus. Historians are still not sure how it was built. They know it took five years to complete, that it was dug from opposite sides of the mountain, and that Eupalinos and his team somehow overcame the problem of how they would get the two tunnels to meet. The tunnelers would have missed by a few feet, but the workers from one side made corrections near the joining place. How could they do this work with primitive tools and weak lamps in deep darkness? One theory is that sunlight from a vertical shaft was bounced off mirrors down the tunnel to give both light and direction.*

◀ A view of Persepolis, center of the Persian Empire, built mainly in the reign of Darius I (c. 520 BCE). The tall stone columns in the middle distance supported decorated wooden ceilings.

**SEE ALSO**

# Aristotle

Aristotle (384–322 BCE) was a Greek philosopher and scientist and one of the most important and influential figures in the history of Western thought. He invented a system of logic that survived to modern times, and his ideas on astronomy – for example, that the sun revolves around the earth – remained the accepted view for the next two thousand years.

## Early Life

Aristotle was born in the Greek colony of Stagira, on the northwest coast of the Aegean Sea. His father, Nicomachus, was the court physician to Amyntas III, king of Macedon. At seventeen Aristotle was sent to Plato's school, the Academy, where he stayed until Plato's death in 347 BCE.

Aristotle's ideas diverged from his teacher's. Plato believed that truth was timeless and unchanging and located not in the physical world but in a superior spiritual existence. Aristotle was too interested in the world to accept that truth was not a part of it.

Some time after leaving the Academy, on the island of Lesbos, Aristotle began his work as a biologist, observing, recording, and classifying marine life in the lagoon of Pyrrha. He established a method of study that he, and later his students, would repeat many times.

▶ *This marble head of Aristotle is owned by the Kunsthistorisches Museum in Vienna. Though some of its features resemble those of other ancient busts of Aristotle, others do not. Thus, it is impossible to know whether any existing work was done by a sculptor who actually saw Aristotle.*

_Surrounded by students, a relatively young Aristotle, in blue, turns to his teacher Plato in the center of this fresco by the sixteenth-century Italian painter Raphael. The fresco is located in the Vatican in Rome._

bled a modern university. Graduates of the school did research under the direction of Aristotle. With his guidance they produced descriptions of the constitutions, or systems of government, of 158 Greek cities. The only one of them to survive is the Constitution of Athens, which has become the main source of information on how Athenian democrocracy worked.

Aristotle's students at the school became known as the Peripatetics, from the Greek words _peri_, "around," and _patein_, "to walk." This name came about because of Aristotle's habit of walking up and down while lecturing.

## Aristotle's Writings

Aristotle wrote on an enormous range of subjects, representing almost every field of knowledge. These subjects included logic, ethics, politics, rhetoric, poetry, biology, psychology, and physics.

Only about one fifth of Aristotle's books – about thirty – have survived. Those most often studied nowadays are _Politics_, which looks at different forms of government, such as democracy and tyranny, and _Poetics_, which is about different kinds of literature, especially tragic plays and epics like Homer's _Iliad_ and _Odyssey_.

Other works, which survive in the form of lecture notes arranged as books, include _Physics_, _On the Heavens_, _History of Animals_, and _Ethics_. In _Ethics_, Aristotle discusses what is good and bad. Happiness is the greatest good, he says, and then asks, what is happiness? Happiness is living in agreement with virtue, and virtue is the halfway point between extremes. He gives other, similar examples: bravery, says Aristotle, is midway between recklessness and timidity, while generosity is halfway between meanness and extravagance.

## Alexander's Tutor

In 342 BCE Aristotle became tutor to the thirteen-year-old son of King Philip II of Macedon, the future Alexander the Great. Aristotle encouraged Alexander to take an interest in the natural world. He also stirred in him a love of literature. Alexander is said to have taken on his travels a copy of Homer's _Iliad_, which Aristotle edited, and to have sent biological specimens to his former tutor from Asia.

## The Lyceum

In 335 BCE in Athens, Aristotle opened the Lyceum, a school that in some ways resem-

In the following passage, taken from Aristotle's *Politics*, he discusses the importance of music as a part of a person's education:

*Men argue that music should be part of education not because it is necessary, because it is not, or because it is useful in the way that writing and reading are useful for business and household affairs. They don't suggest that music helps you as a future citizen the way drawing can help you to judge a vase or a piece of sculpture you might buy, or the way physical education contributes to health and a vigorous life. Music does not lead to obvious benefits such as these. There is only one reason for learning music, and that is because it is a civilized pursuit for free people with leisure.*

▼ An extract from the only surviving copy of Aristotle's "Athenian Constitution," written on an Egyptian papyrus around 100 CE. Aristotle's students contributed to this work. A professional library scribe would have copied it.

## Criminal Charges

After Alexander's death in 323 BCE, there was much anti-Macedonian feeling in Athens. Aristotle, now sixty-one, was charged, like Socrates before him, with antireligious teaching and behavior – a criminal offense. He left Athens, and in 322 he died in the city of Chalcis close by.

## Conclusion

Although many of Aristotle's ideas are now out of date, in other ways he remains surprisingly modern. He made the first scientific studies in biology and zoology, observing and recording in detail the lives of marine and land creatures and classifying what he had recorded. He used the same scientific approach in subjects ranging from poetry to politics. To modern scholars he is now of greater interest as a philosopher, with his arguments for the existence of God and his use of a system of logic to explain how the universe works.

### SEE ALSO
- Alexander the Great • Athens • Greece
- Greek Mythology • Greek Philosophy
- Plato • Science • Socrates

# Art

Making beautiful objects simply for people's enjoyment was very rare in ancient times. The ancient Greeks, who made many beautiful objects, did not have a word for art. They used the word *techne*, from which the word *technical* is derived, to refer to many skills, from writing a poem or making a pot to laying out an orchard or building a ship. Similarly, in ancient Egypt very few artists are known by name because their work was seen as simply fulfilling a function and not significant in its own right.

### Art and Magic

In ancient times craftspeople intended the objects they made to have a definite use. Some uses were magical. A cave painting of an animal magically helped the hunt; the animal was "captured" first by representing it as a picture. Painted or sculpted animals often had a protective function. For example, the lions at the Gate of Malatya in ninth century BCE Turkey and the winged bulls carved with human heads at the doors of Sargon's palace in Assyria in the eighth century BCE were regarded as magical guardians of those places.

In ancient Greece craftsmen were believed to perform magic when they made objects that looked like living things. What was lifelike might come to life. Hephaestos,

▼ This wall painting of a deer being captured, from Çatal Hüyük, in Turkey, was made between about 6850 and 6300 BCE.

the mythical Greek god of *techne*, made tables for the gods that moved on their own. Greek comedies refer to statues that walk or are chained down to prevent them from running away. Below a statue of a heifer by the sculptor Myron, on the Athenian Acropolis, there is an inscription: "I am Myron's little heifer. Drive me along, herdsman, drive me off to the herd."

## Art and Religion

Ancient art often had a religious purpose. A stone figurine found in Mohenjo Daro in India is probably a representation of a priest from a family altar. Sculptures of Buddha and bodhisattvas were intended to promote calm and to dispel greed and earthly longing. In ancient Greece the giant statue of Zeus at Olympia represented the terrifying and protective god in residence. The Nasca people of inland Peru drew huge animals on the desert floor for religious reasons — perhaps as a gift to the gods to seek their protection.

In Egypt scenes were painted on the walls of tombs portraying a perfect world – the afterlife – in which the tomb owner lived happily, surrounded by courtiers and servants. In one painting, in the tomb of Pashedu at Thebes, the dead man is shown drinking from a pool at the foot of a date palm.

▼ This painting from an Egyptian tomb, dating from around 2500–2350 BCE, shows the dead person seated in front of a table laden with the food he needed in the afterlife.

## Art as a Public Record

Much ancient art, in societies where few people were able to read, functioned in various ways as a public record. Art was information in painted or sculpted form. Objects now defined as art often had this practical purpose initially.

For example, the impressive-looking Moche heads from the coast of Peru, created around 200 CE, were designed not to please but to preserve the memory of certain people. A famous Assyrian relief that shows King Tiglath-pileser III (745–727 BCE) directing a battle from his chariot records a piece of history and celebrates the king's role in it. Another relief shows trade or diplomacy in action, as two Phoenicians present the Assyrian king Ashurnasirpal with tribute that includes two carved monkeys.

Painting and sculpture sometimes depicted typical daily life. The frescoes of cattle and herdsmen in the caves of Tassili in the Sahara, painted around 1000 BCE, were for these people not works of art but a vivid record of how their society functioned.

Art was also an important way of retelling important myths and stories. The most popular myths of ancient Greece were retold in paintings and scuptures. This art appeared on pottery, on walls, in temples, and in public buildings. Similarly, the murals in the caves of Ajanta in India, dating from around 400 CE, were paintings that retold instructive stories.

## Art and Leisure

Ancient art does not always appear to have a definite purpose, however. Some early art seems to exist, like modern painting or sculpture, to add to the enjoyment of public and private spaces. In an ancient Greek house in Akrotiri on the island of Thera, there is a fresco of a young girl gathering crocuses, painted for no other reason than to beautify a room. Egyptian tombs are also full of beautiful images of houses and gardens, but these images also had a functional purpose and were believed to magically sustain the dead through eternity.

◄ This fine Moche head, made between 600 and 400 BCE on the coast of Peru, is probably of a real person of importance. The headdress and extended earlobes indicate a person of high status, as do the strongly individual features of the face.

# GREEK BRONZE SCULPTURE

In the sixth century BCE Greek craftsmen discovered a way of making hollow sculptures using bronze. Previously, wood and stone had been the only materials used for Greek sculptures. Bronze had advantages over stone, which was expensive and might split and fracture even in the quarry. Poses that were impossible in stone, because of its weight, could be achieved with bronze. The process was also more flexible and convenient. Bronze sculptures were lighter to carry and unlikely to break on rough sea journeys. Parts could be made separately and joined together. Hair could be changed to suit individual figures. Ornaments, such as earrings or gold headbands, could be fixed on after the sculpture was made. Eyes and teeth of silver or tin could be inserted.

Bronze soon became very popular among sculptors. The process of creating sculptures was made more efficient, with the result that bronze sculptures could be produced not just one at a time but in numbers. Some famous sculptures may have been produced this way, for example, a pair of sculptures found in the sea near Riace in Italy and a figure of Zeus found in the sea near Cape Sounion, southwest of Athens.

The development of bronze sculpture shows the clear connection between techne and art in ancient Greece. With bronze, craftsmen were trying out new techniques that led to major advances in Greek art.

*A bronze sculpture of a Greek woman athlete from the sixth century BCE, perhaps from Sparta.*

故曰翼翼矜矜福所以興靜恭自思榮顯所期

歡不可以瀆寵不可以專實生慢愛則極遷致盈必損理有固然美者自美翩以取尤冶容求好君子所以沈結恩而絕寔此之由

▲ This is an illustration from a fourth-century-CE booklet of advice for ladies of the Chinese royal court, written by one known as the Instructress. The painter, thought to be Gu Kaizhi, born in 345 CE, used ink and color on a silk scroll.

Gradually there developed, at different times in different civilizations, a sense that beautiful objects had a value in their own right. The Greek architects of the Parthenon in Athens thought as artists, building slight curves, swellings, and narrowings into their design so that the building would seem airy and appear to float and not sit too heavily on the earth.

Evidence of such changes in attitude comes from writings, too. One example is the Chinese artist of the fourth century CE who wrote that he tried in his paintings to "portray the spirit through the form" – a phrase that might sum up the aim of many modern artists.

### SEE ALSO

- Acropolis • Athens • Buddhism • China
- Egypt • Greek Mythology • Knossos
- Mohenjo Daro

## POLYGNOTOS OF THASOS

Polygnotos is the most famous painter from ancient Greece. He was born on Thasos and worked in Athens between about 470 and 450 BCE. His patron was the politician Cimon, who was responsible for much of the rebuilding needed in Athens after its destruction by the Persians in 479 BCE. Through Cimon, Polygnotos first worked on the Painted Stoa, a covered walkway in Athens covered in paintings of Athenian military victories. Later, at Delphi, he produced two murals, *The Fall of Troy* and *Odysseus's Visit to the Underworld*. Both were very large, with dozens of figures on a surface about 15 feet (4.6 m) high. Polygnotos's Delphi paintings were a great success, and he was rewarded with free food and lodging for life. The Roman writer Pliny the Elder said that Polygnotos was the first painter to show faces with the mouth open and teeth visible and the first to paint women in transparent drapery.

# Aryans

By the middle of the second millennium BCE, a people calling themselves Arya, or "noble ones," were living in northwest India. Historians call these people Aryans. The Aryans' closest relatives were the ancient Iranians, as their similar name suggests. Aryans and Iranians were probably the same people at one time, living as nomads and moving with herds of cattle across the dry plains of central Asia. At some point they separated, and the Aryans moved south into India.

Research has not uncovered evidence showing when the Aryans reached their new homeland, though there are many different theories. Some scholars believe that they arrived toward the end of the Indus valley civilization, around 2000 BCE, and may have conquered some of the Indus cities. Others argue that they came later, only after those cities had fallen into ruin.

The Aryans first settled in the Punjab, the plain where five rivers flow into the Indus. They lived in small villages, still raising cattle but now also growing crops, such as barley, using a plow pulled by an ox. They later spread east, reaching the valley of India's other great river, the Ganges, in the first millennium BCE.

## Vedas

The source of almost all current knowledge about the mysterious Aryans is their collection of religious poems, the Vedas. These are thought to date from between 1700 and 900 BCE and are the oldest Indian texts that can be understood.

For many hundreds of years, the Vedas were memorized and passed on by word of mouth. It was not until a new writing system was invented, sometime after 500 BCE, that they were written down. The Vedas are so important that the whole of Indian history between around 1700 and 500 BCE is known as the Vedic period.

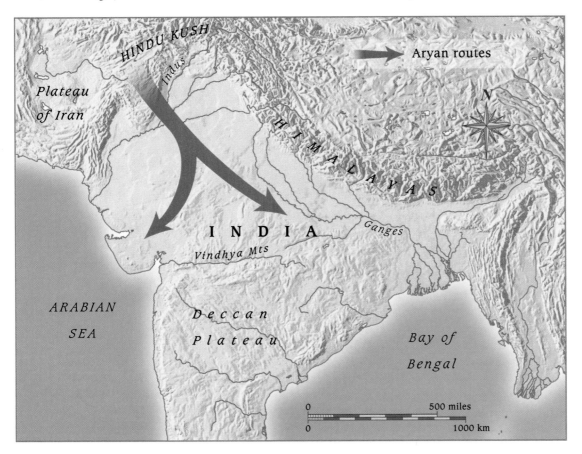

◀ At an unknown date before 1500 BCE, the Aryans crossed into India from their original homeland to the northwest.

## Society

According to the Vedas the first Aryans lived in *janas*, or clans – tribes whose members all believed they were descended from a single ancestor. Each clan was ruled by a chief called a *raja*, a word that later came to mean "king."

Over time, four different classes developed. At the top were the Brahmans, or priests. Next were the Kshatriya – the nobles and warriors. Below them were the Vaisya – craftspeople and merchants. At the bottom were the Sudra, or servants and laborers. These designations are thought by many scholars to be the beginning of the caste system, the division of Indian society into classes, whose members would only marry others from their own caste.

## Warfare

The Aryans were a warlike people who rode into battle on horse-drawn chariots, shooting arrows at their enemies. In early times fighting took the form of cattle raids. The Aryan word for war, *gavisti*, means "searching for cattle." Later, the aim of warfare was to conquer territory.

## Religion

The Aryans worshiped many gods, who were thought to provide all the good things in life – victory in war, wealth, cattle, and "heroic sons." The most powerful god was Indra, the sky and war god. People pictured him riding a chariot across the sky armed with a thunderbolt, smashing the clouds open and releasing the rain.

Other important gods were Agni, the fire god, Mitra, the sun god, and his brother Varuna, who was god of the moon and lord of the dead. Varuna also had a special role as a god who watched over oaths.

In order to win the gods' favor, the Brahmans performed ceremonies in which they praised the gods by reciting the Vedas and offered them sacrifices. Cattle, horses,

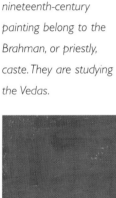

▼ The boys in this nineteenth-century painting belong to the Brahman, or priestly, caste. They are studying the Vedas.

# SANSKRIT

The best evidence that the Aryans were not originally from India is that their language, Sanskrit, is closely related to most of the languages of Europe and western Asia. The word ignite, *for example, comes from the Latin word for "fire,"* ignis, *which is very similar to* agni, *the Aryans' word for "fire" and the name of their fire god.*

*Vocabulary provides other evidence that the Aryans did not come from India. Aryans had to invent a name for the elephant, calling it "the beast with a hand." As elephants were common Indian animals, the lack of an Aryan name suggests that their language developed in a land without elephants.*

| ARYANS |
|---|

**c. 20,000–17,000 BCE**

End of the Indus valley civilization.

**c. 17,000–c. 800 BCE**

Early Vedic period. Aryan clans living in the Punjab. Change from nomadic life to settled village communities.

**c. 800–c. 500 BCE**

Later Vedic period. Aryans move east into the Ganges valley. Rise of different classes. Ironworking is introduced. The formation of the first kingdoms occurs.

▲ *Indra, the most powerful Aryan god, is shown in this wall painting from the seventh or eighth century CE.*

and sometimes even people were killed as offerings to the gods. The sacrificial offering was burned on a movable brick altar. Agni, the fire god, was thought to eat the meat, turning it into smoke, which then rose to feed the other gods.

## Kingdoms

By the fifth century BCE the Aryans had established a number of kingdoms across northern India. The kingdoms were ruled by rajas, who held elaborate ceremonies in which they gave large amounts of wealth away to their Brahmans and nobles.

The most famous ceremony held by the rajas was the *aswamedha*, or horse sacrifice. A specially chosen horse was released and allowed to roam freely for a year. It was followed by a group of soldiers who kept track of its route. Any lands that the horse wandered across were then claimed by the king, who believed that the horse's journey was a sign sent by the gods. At the end of the year, the horse was recaptured and sacrificed.

### Archaeology

Unlike the Indus cities, the Aryan kingdoms have left very little for archaeologists to dig up, because the Aryans did not build in fired brick. Even their royal palaces were made of timber and mud, which leave little trace behind.

What does survive in great quantities is pottery, particularly a type called painted gray ware, which is found in many areas that the Aryans settled. However, it is impossible to prove that this pottery was actually made by the Aryans, who were only one of many peoples of ancient India.

▼ *This page is from a Sanskrit book dating from the 1750s CE. It is written in Brahmi script, the writing system invented some time after 500 BCE. All modern Indian writing systems, as well as many in South Asia, are based on Brahmi.*

A DESCRIPTION IN THE VEDAS OF INDRA, THE SKY AND WAR GOD:

The one in whose control are horses,
cows, villages, all chariots
The one who has caused to be born
the sun, the dawn
The one who is the waters' leader
He, oh people, is Indra . . .
The one without whom people do
not conquer,
The one to whom, when fighting,
they call for help,
The one who is a match for
everyone,
The one who shakes the unshakable
He, oh people, is Indra.

**SEE ALSO**

• Hinduism • Indian Philosophy
• Indus Valley

# Glossary

**amphitheater** An oval, open-air space surrounded by seating, used for public entertainments.

**antiquarian** A person who collects old objects.

**artifact** An ancient object made by humans; often one that comes to light through archaeological research.

**bodhisattva** According to Buddhist teaching, a being who has attained enlightenment but remains in the human world to help others.

**citadel** A fortress or stronghold built to defend a city.

**concubine** A woman who lives with a wealthy man, especially a king, without being his wife.

**consul** The leader of the Roman senate. A senior and junior consul were elected every year.

**crop mark** The pattern made in a field by the different ways in which a crop grows over buried walls, ditches, and pits. A crop growing above a wall will have shallow roots, and it will dry out sooner than a crop growing above a ditch or a pit, where the roots can reach deeper into the ground for moisture. Seen from the air, crop marks above walls appear light in color; those above ditches and pits appear dark.

**dendrochronology** A dating method in which the annual growth rings of a piece of timber are matched against a master chart to produce a date that equates to the year in which the timber was felled.

**didgeridoo** An aboriginal musical instrument consisting of a long thick wooden pipe that the player blows into, creating a deep humming sound.

**epic** A long poem describing the adventures and deeds of a legendary hero or heroes.

**fresco** Wall painting where paint is applied to fresh damp plaster.

**galley** A long, low-lying boat propelled by oars or sails, used in ancient times, especially in the Mediterranean.

**heifer** A young cow, especially one that has never had a calf.

**mercenaries** Professional soldiers paid to fight for an army other than that of their country.

**Minerva** The Roman goddess of handicrafts, the arts, the professions and war.

**mortuary temple** A temple built near the tomb of a dead person where prayers were said and where offerings could be made. In the case of pharaohs (and one or two nonpharaohs), they were also worshiped as gods.

**mural** A large picture painted directly onto a wall.

**pacify** Bring to a state of peace.

**pastoral** Presenting a happy image of country life.

**patron** Somebody who gives money or other support to someone else.

**potassium-argon dating** A dating method based on the rate of decay of the isotope potassium 40 to argon 40.

**potsherd** A fragment of pottery, especially one found at an archaeological site.

**Praetorian Guard** The emperor's personal bodyguard, numbering several thousand soldiers with two commanders.

**radiocarbon dating** A dating method that relies on the fact that carbon 14, a radioactive isotope present in all living things, decays at a known rate, enabling fixed points in time to be calculated.

**refugee** A person seeking a safe place to live while escaping from war or persecution.

**satrap** The noble governor of a district in the Persian empire.

**senate** A legislative body, such as that of ancient Rome.

**stoa** In ancient Greece, a covered walkway, usually with a row of columns on one side and a wall on the other.

**stratigraphy** Layers, or strata, of an archaeological site.

**thread pump** A screw inserted in a watertight tube that, when turned, draws up water in the spiral of its thread.

**tuberculosis** A disease of the lungs that can lead to death.

**vassal** A person, nation, or group that is dominated or occupied by another ruler or nation.

# Index

Page numbers in **boldface type** refer to main articles. Page numbers in *italic type* refer to illustrations.